A Handbook of Costume Drawing

Second Edition

A Handbook
of Costume Drawing

A Guide to Drawing the Period Figure for Costume Design Students

Second Edition

Georgia O'Daniel Baker

Illustrated by
Helen Redel Pullen

**Focal
Press**

Boston Oxford Auckland Johannesburg Melbourne New Delhi

Focal Press is an imprint of Butterworth–Heinemann.

Copyright © 2000 by Butterworth–Heinemann

 A member of the Reed Elsevier group

 Recognizing the importance of preserving what has been written, Butterworth–Heinemann prints its books on acid-free paper whenever possible.

 Butterworth–Heinemann supports the efforts of American Forests and the Global ReLeaf program in its campaign for the betterment of trees, forests, and our environment.

Cover credit: Color costume designs by Georgia O'Daniel Baker. Additional black and white line drawings reprinted with the permission of Scribner, a division of Simon & Schuster from *The Mode in Footwear* and *The Mode in Hats and Headdresses* by R. Turner Wilcox. Copyright 1948, 1946 by Charles Scribner's Sons; copyright renewed © 1976 by Ruth Wilcox; and *Racinet's Full-Color Pictorial History of Western Costume* by Auguste Racinet, Dover Publications, 1988; originally published by the Librairie de Firmin-Didot et Cie, Paris, 1888.

Library of Congress Cataloging-in-Publication Data
Baker, Georgia O'Daniel.
    A handbook of costume drawing : a guide to drawing the period figure for costume design students / Georgia O'Daniel Baker ; illustrated by Helen Redel Pullen.—2nd ed.
    p.   cm.
Includes bibliographical references and index.
ISBN 0-240-80403-1 (pbk. : alk. paper)
    1. Fashion drawing.   2. Costume design.   I. Title.

TT509.B35   2000
741.6'72--dc21   99-087664

British Library Cataloguing-in-Publication Data
A catalogue record for this book is available from the British Library.

The publisher offers special discounts on bulk orders of this book.
For information, please contact:

Manager of Special Sales
Butterworth–Heinemann
225 Wildwood Avenue
Woburn, MA 01801-2041
Tel: 781-904-2500
Fax: 781-904-2620

For information on all Focal Press publications available, contact our World Wide Web home page at: http://www.focalpress.com

10 9 8 7 6 5 4 3 2 1

Printed in the United States of America

To my children Caroline and Christopher, who have created with me a family of warmth, support, challenge, negotiation, growth, and love.

G. O'D.B.

For the loving support of my parents, Helen Mueller Redel and Milford Lawrence Redel, and my son Anthony Alexander Pullen.

H. R. P.

Contents

Preface

Clothes may or may not "make" the man or woman. However, clothes do change the shape of the human body through the different periods of costume history. The purpose of this book is to help the students of costume design and costume history do what Ingham and Covey call "seeing accurately." By seeing how fashion changes the human form to create a "desirable" shape or image for an historical period, they can more easily make the transition from a contemporary look to a period silhouette in costume research and sketching. These period images can be utilized to create the "mood" of a play or playwright.

This text looks at changes from a "normal" silhouette to the waist, neck, shoulders, arms, and hemlines throughout costume history. Whatever "beauty" is in the eye of the current beholder, it is always affected by the look of the clothing silhouette today and in the past.

Each historical period illustrates how the period look is often created by constricting or adding to the body in some manner. Large clothed male and female figures appear in each section dressed in some of the major garments from this period. The text and drawings make every effort to present a clear and easy-to-"read" figure for the student learning to draw a period costume.

Adjacent to the large figure are detail drawings of hairstyles, footwear, undergarments, neckwear, and often accessories from that historical period. Of course, there are many types and items of dress that have not been included. This is just one silhouette typical of the period. The hope is that by seeing this silhouette clearly you may more easily draw this silhouette or others from this period. The text tries to give a clear description of major garments from each period, but does not try to be comprehensive in covering all aspects of costume history.

The style of artwork in each section reflects the dominant rendering style of that period. The faces, shape of the figure, pose, posture, and hairstyles are designed to convey the mood or feeling of the period.

This book has evolved after years of teaching costume history and costume design to students without fine arts training but with a desire to learn to draw and design costumes. Seeing a period costume clearly makes learning to draw easier. This book aims to make drawing period clothing easier and more enjoyable.

Georgia O'Daniel Baker

A principal aim of this book is the presentation of visuals which will help the designer produce images reflective of a period and its mood. To that end, the drawings are based upon characteristic renderings of the time.

The introduction of details in Chapter 1, such as eyes, ears, gathers, and pleats-mysteries to most beginning designers-has been included to help the student reach the goal of a clearly presented idea.

Helen Redel Pullen

Acknowledgments

My appreciation to those who have helped me create a joyous and satisfying career in costume design: Doug Russell for his unwavering standards of excellence and his personal integrity. Teachers and mentors Herb Camburn, Tanya Moiseiwitsch, Paul Berman, C. Richard Gillespie. Cheryl Partridge, who makes the costumes come alive on stage. Judy Dolan, Sheila Kehoe, William Crowther, Marianne Wittelsberger, Steve Bauer, and the many students who inspire and energize me as professional colleagues and friends. And to my parents who always valued and encouraged education.

Georgia O'Daniel Baker
Baltimore, Maryland

As an educator and artist, it has been exciting to develop a project one hopes will be of value to students. Of the many colleagues and friends whose support and advice has been important to me, I would particularly like to thank Bernadine Basile, Jocelyn Curtis, George Fondersmith, and Jane Warth.

Helen Redel Pullen

Chapter 1

The Basic Figure
and How Clothes Fit the Body

The Figure

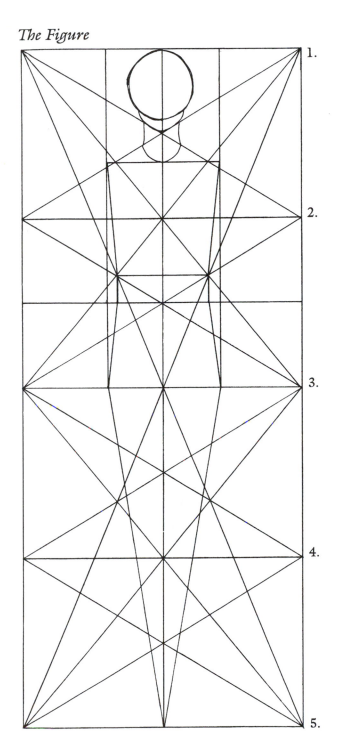

Female *Male*

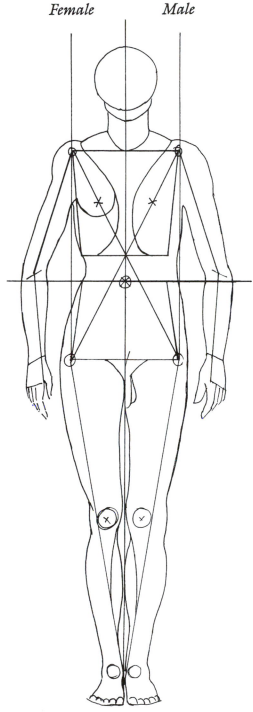

Figure 1.1 This diagram shows a method of arriving at correct proportions for the human figure using a rectangle to show proportions of the width and length of the figure.

Figure 1.2 A correctly proportioned male and female figure using the specifications established in Figure 1.1. The hip hits at the center line of the rectangle, line #3. Line #2 is the center line of the chest or bustline. Line #4 is at the knee.

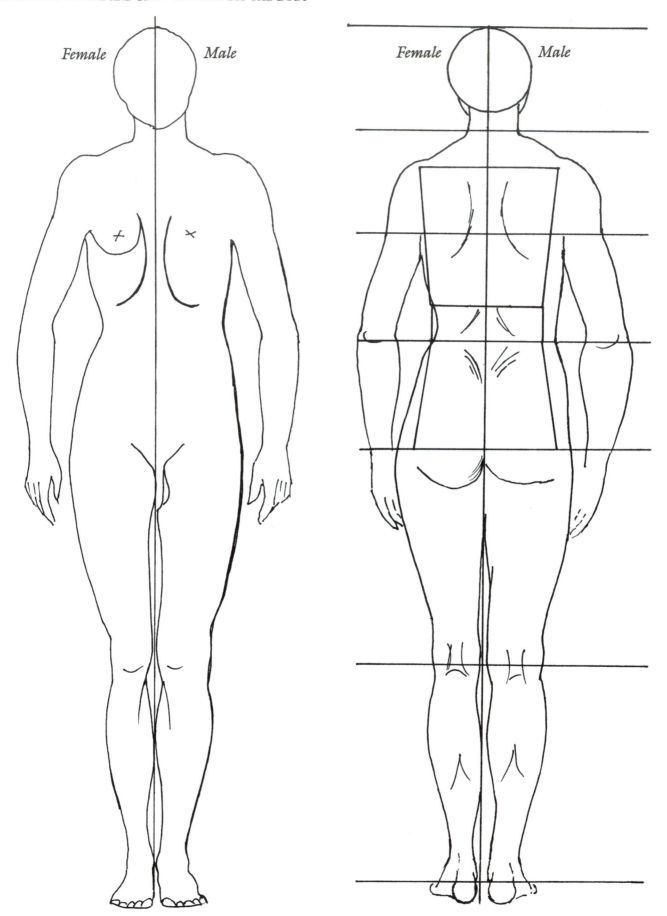

Figure 1.3 a. One-half of each the male and female figures without the box structure. b. The back view.

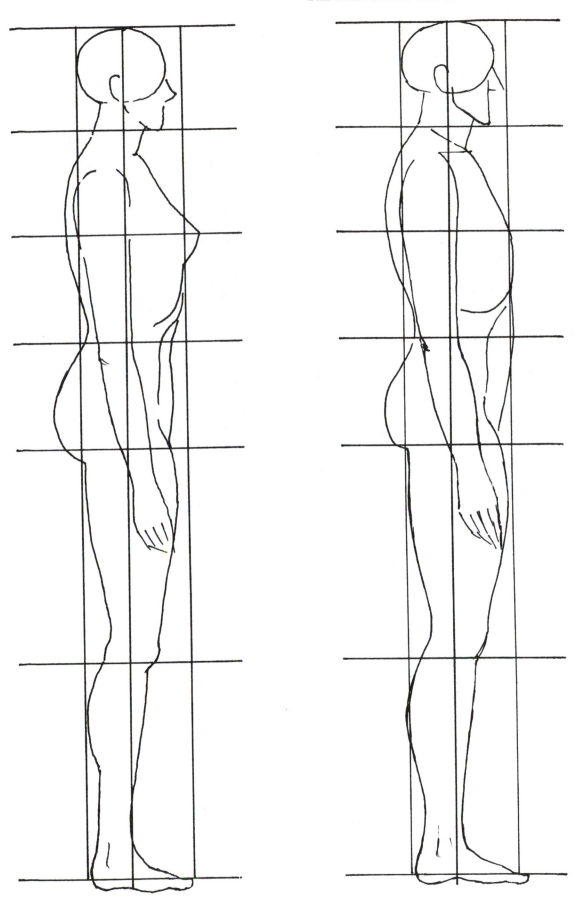

Figure 1.4 An illustration of the body proportions from a side view of the female and male figure.

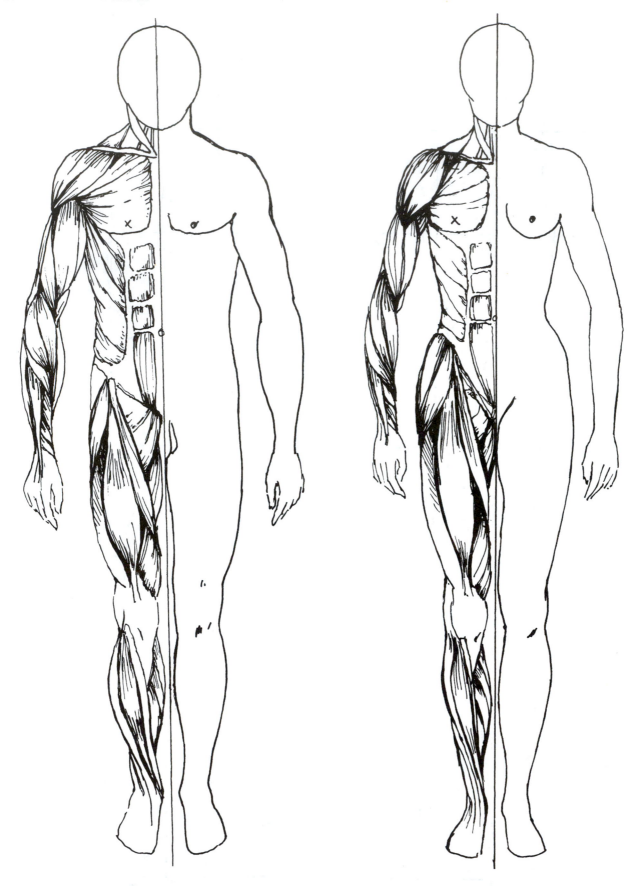

Figure 1.5 The muscle structure of the male body illustrating the thicker neck and shoulder muscles, a wider waist, narrower hip, and more developed thigh muscles.

The female muscle structure constitutes a thinner neck, bust point at the armpit, narrower waist, and fuller hips.

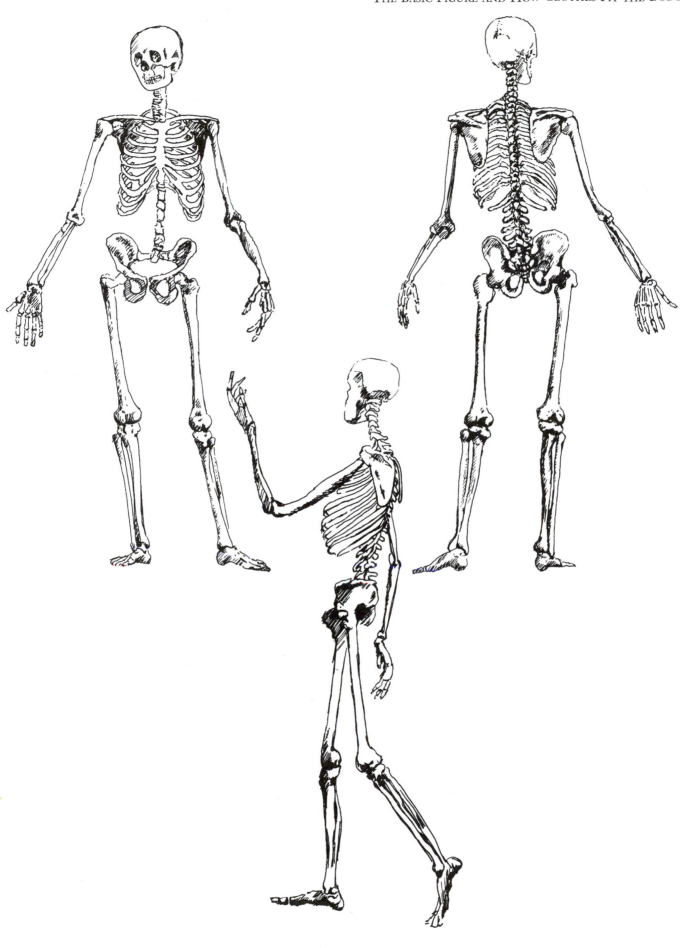

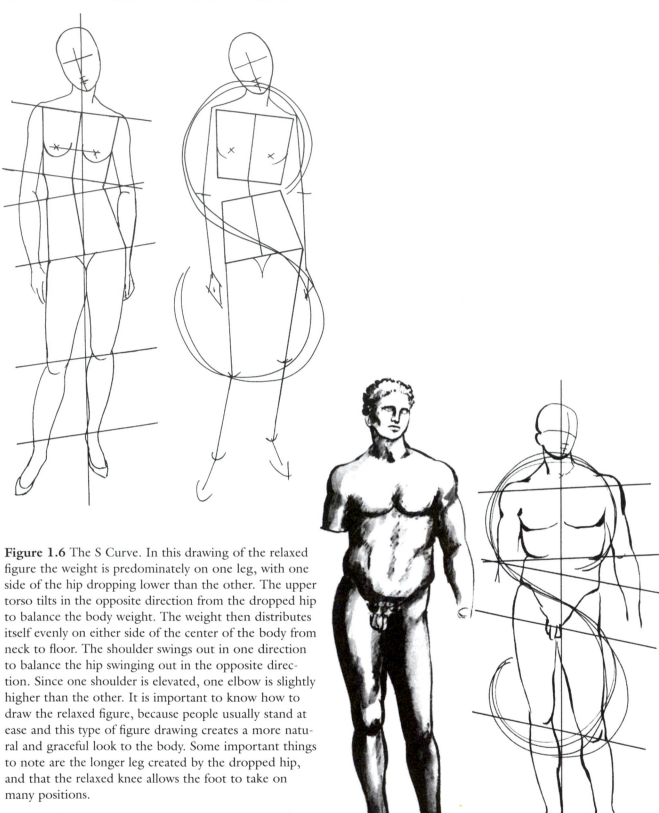

Figure 1.6 The S Curve. In this drawing of the relaxed figure the weight is predominately on one leg, with one side of the hip dropping lower than the other. The upper torso tilts in the opposite direction from the dropped hip to balance the body weight. The weight then distributes itself evenly on either side of the center of the body from neck to floor. The shoulder swings out in one direction to balance the hip swinging out in the opposite direction. Since one shoulder is elevated, one elbow is slightly higher than the other. It is important to know how to draw the relaxed figure, because people usually stand at ease and this type of figure drawing creates a more natural and graceful look to the body. Some important things to note are the longer leg created by the dropped hip, and that the relaxed knee allows the foot to take on many positions.

Figure 1.7 The relaxed figure as it is first seen in Greek sculpture.

The Face

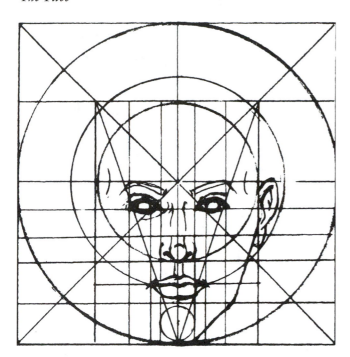

Figure 1.8 The value of the square diagram is to show the regularity of the human face. It can be divided horizontally at the one-half point to easily place the eyebrows. The top quarter mark is the bottom of the nose. The bottom eighth marks the cleft in the chin, and halfway between the cleft and the bottom of the nose marks the line of the lips.

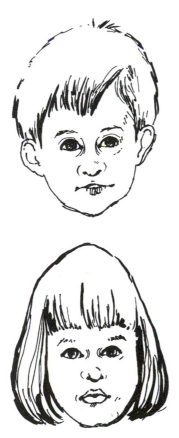

Figure 1.9 The female and male face, front view, based on the square diagram showing placement of the features. The male face has a wider jawline, thinner mouth, and more pronounced nose bridge. The eyebrows are thicker and less arched.

Figure 1.10 The child's face is smaller in relationship to the skull. The proportion of a child's head to the body is one to four. The eyes are the same as the adult, but the nose and mouth are smaller.

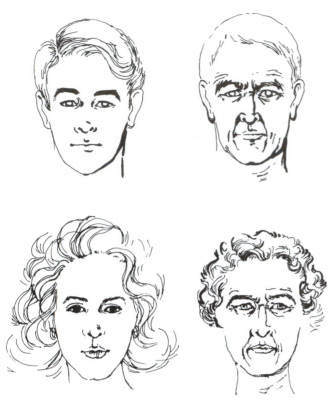

Figure 1.13 Illustrations of different treatments and ways to indicate front views of the eye and eyebrow for males and females.

Figure 1.11 A contrast of youthful faces with aging faces. In the aging faces eyebrows are shaggier and hair thins. Muscles lose elasticity, creating folds above and below the eye socket area. The nasal labial fold starts in the bottom fold of the nose and ends just above the mouth. Small folds appear on the forehead and around the mouth.

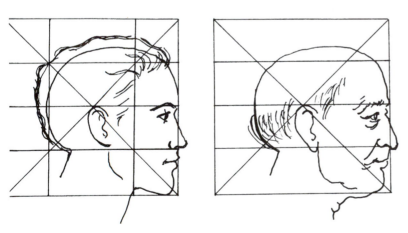

Figure 1.12 The grid on the profile of the face shows the correct placement of the ear. The one-quarter vertical line on the left marks the back of the skull. The one-quarter vertical line on the right marks the placement of the jawline at the bottom of the face.

Figure 1.14 Profile of eyes and eyebrows.

Figure 1.15 A three-quarter view of the face. Note the eyes and eyebrows, as well as how the straight hair is drawn.

Figure 1.16 Wavy hair.

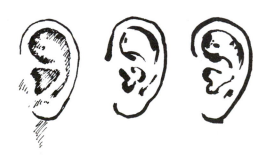

Figure 1.18 It is important when drawing the mouth to indicate the line between the two lips, the expression line, and the bottom or top lip.

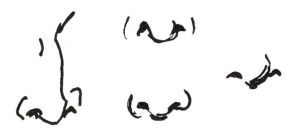

Figure 1.17 Simple ways of indicating the shape of the nose. Sometimes only the tip of the nose will be enough to create the whole look.

Figure 1.19 A side view of an ear.

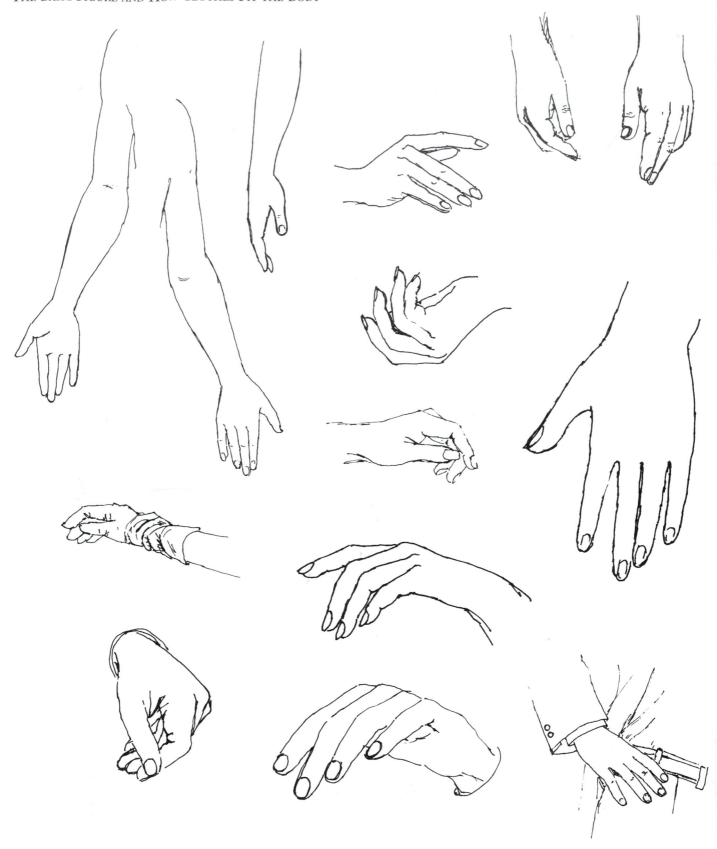

Figure 1.20 A variety of relaxed hands showing front, back, and side positions. Additional views include the hand on the hip, gloved, and several ways of drawing a relaxed, partially closed hand.

The Foot

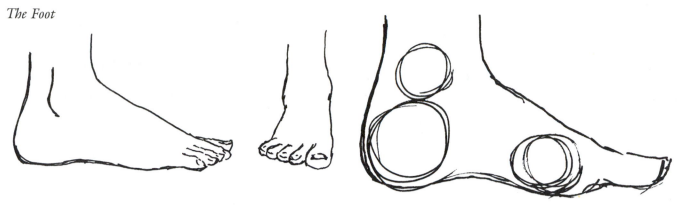

Figure 1.21 Barefoot poses from the front and the side.

Figure 1.22 The large bone structure of the foot.

Figure 1.23 Various shoes, boots, flat heels, and high heels.

Detail Drawing for Creating Realistic Clothing on the Human Body.

Figure 1.24 It is important to remember that clothing doesn't lie flat on the human body. Instead, it curves and follows the natural curve of the figure. Notice how the cuff curves around the wrist at both the top and bottom of the cuff; how both the wrist and arm can be thought of as a cylinder; and how the fabric folds in the bent sleeve of the elbow, showing the movement of the fabric as the arm is placed on the hip. Cloth also folds and curves when coming in contact with other clothing. Observe how the sleeve curves as it sets into a jacket or blouse.

Figure 1.26 When the clothing is belted at the waist, folds may appear in the fabric above and below the waistline.

Figure 1.27 An indication of how the crown of the head fits into the hat to create a more accurate look where the hat brim hits the forehead.

Figure 1.25 An example of how the collar curves as it goes around the neck.

Figure 1.29 When drawing a hemline going around the body, note the depth of the vertical folds and how they get shorter as they go around to the side and back of the body.

Figure 1.28 One way of drawing gathers or ruffles in fabric.

Figure 1.30 Two illustrations of how to draw patterning on fabric. Note that the pattern does not need to cover the complete garment to capture the look of checked or plaid patterning. Spaces can be left out as they are in the diamond-shaped patterning in the skirt. Where highlights would hit the skirt, the pattern would appear to be less detailed.

Figure 1.31 Usually, inexperienced artists draw something resembling a comic book illustration, lacking any subtlety of line. Common mistakes that students often make include drawing the heads too large with wide and staring eyes. The lips have a heavy definition with a straight line separating them. Hair is often either too complex or too simple. Hands and feet are too small and the clothing seems pasted onto the body. The figure seems to float, not stand on any real surface.

Figure 1.32 An example of a wash on a figure to create a more three-dimensional effect. The wide wash of diluted black India ink down the left side of the clothing creates a shadow and highlight effect on the figure. Smaller shadows are on the right sleeve, on the collar, and in the fold of the skirt. This helps to create a stronger sense of reality and movement in the clothing.

Figure 1.33 An India ink wash creates a shadow at the left side and bottom of the figure. A parquet wood floor treatment is at the right.

Figure 1.35 The gentleman stands on a stone walk with a hint of wrought iron fence and a tree.

Figure 1.34 A more abstracted India ink wash. For beginners, note these take practice to perfect. Initially, use a photocopy of the illustration and practice washes until they look natural. The plant stand, floral arrangement, and carpeting effect create the mood of an 1870s room.

Figure 1.36 This gentleman is "grounded" by a few lines indicating a floor or walk.

Figure 1.37 An example of a floor and background wash. Costume sketch for *The Devil's Disciple* by Sheila Kehoe

Chapter *2*

Materials and Techniques

In learning about media for drawing and painting costume sketches, it is important to try varieties of media and find one you are comfortable using. It needs to be a style of drawing and rendering that you can use with speed, flexibility, and a high level of artistic skill. Below are some of the media with which you will want to be familiar.

Pencils

Sketching starts with pencils. It is important to start with a 4B or 6B drawing pencil and a pencil sharpener of some type. The softer leads of these pencils make drawing easier and more fluid. You need to keep your pencils sharpened so the line you draw is the line you want. To a beginner this may not seem important to the quality and accuracy of your drawing, but it is. If you can afford an electric pencil sharpener, it is a great convenience. If not, use a manual sharpener available in art supply stores at nominal cost. In addition to sketching, pencils are used to add detail to finished watercolor sketches to sharpen the image as a final step in completing the costume rendering. Prismacolor pencils can also be used for drawing as well as for coloring sketches. They are especially useful for mixing flesh tones.

Inks

Preliminary sketches are made in pencil, and it is useful to photocopy them for experimenting with ink and watercolor. You can also draw on top of the original sketch. Going over sketches in permanent black, gray, or sepia India ink gives them additional clarity. You can add ink washes for shadow effects. Ink drawing is easiest with a regular fountain pen or a crow-quill pen. It will take a little practice to get used to the feel of the pen and the flow of the ink if you are a beginner.

Colored inks can be used alone to create saturated colors if you need bright hues. They do not mix as easily as watercolors with other media because they are alcohol-based instead of water-based. Permanent black, gray, or sepia ink is useful for detailing sketches after you have completed watercolors. It can give the sketch back the clarity it had in pencil form. You can detail lace, buttons, ribbons, jewelry, feathers, pleats, gathers, and trimmings.

Permanent-ink washes can be used to create shadows, pleats, and other effects such as aging and distressing of fabrics. This may be added either before or after you color the sketches. Washes done in light, medium, and dark gray can add a strong three-dimensional quality to figures and fabrics. Since the ink is permanent, water does not affect it, and it can be applied either under or over watercolors. Photocopy a few sketches and experiment with ink washes to get the effect of shadows coming from a light source. It is usually easiest to work left to right with the darkest shadows at the left of the figure and the highlight or light source on the right. It is important to find a way to sketch and render that is comfortable and easy for you. Since costume designers do many sketches, a quick and easy technique is essential.

Watercolors

By far the most flexible medium for costume rendering is watercolor. Watercolor includes both opaque watercolor paints, called *gouache* or *casein*, and transparent watercolors such as Windsor Newton, Grumbacher Brilliant Symphonic, or Pelikan. Watercolors can be applied in thick or thin layers, creating the feeling of different textures. They mix easily with other watercolors and with other media to create a wide range of hues, values, and saturations in color. The Grumbacher Brilliant watercolor set is arranged in the same pattern as the color wheel and is especially easy for beginners to use.

When beginning to work with watercolors, use a white plate to mix paints and to add water to pigment. Keep an extra sheet of white paper to test colors before you try them on your sketches. Adding less water results in more opaque and more saturated colors. Adding more water creates pastels and transparent colors. It is efficient to have a small tube of white and black: they are useful by themselves and also in mixing tints and shades. Flesh tones can be created by mixing tan or brown shades with white, depending on how light or dark you want the skin tones to be. A dot of yellow or blue can sometimes balance out the skin shades. Paints vary greatly in the brown shades available.

After you have mixed a sample of the color on a plate and tested it on a spare piece of paper, you can test it on your sketch. Photocopying two or three extra sketches allows you to work with colors and try different effects while preserving your original pencil sketch for your final color choices. If you work left to right on the figure, you will always have a darker color on one side and a lighter one on the other, creating a natural highlight and shadow effect. You can add a small amount of water as you move to the right to increase this effect. Finding a consistent way to paint that is comfortable for you is important.

It is usually easier to do large areas of color first and to add detail colors later. Be sure to put the sketches aside to let the colors dry before you apply the next color. It is also useful to begin by doing all the flesh tones or all the blacks or whites on several sketches to "warm up" your painting skills. There is a rhythm to painting and drawing. It takes a little time to get into the rhythm. It is similar to a dancer or athlete warming up before dancing or running.

Watercolor Pencils

Watercolor pencils are colored pencils that, when passed over with a wet brush, create a "watercolor" effect. They come in a good range of colors and last a long time. These pencils are especially effective for creating stripes and plaids, floral prints, and patterns, and for adding texture, such as aging and distressing, to costume sketches. They are a quick technique that is useful for preliminary sketches either for laying in color or for details, such as buttons, and accessories such as shoes. It is worth experimenting with the many ways they can be used over

or under watercolor paints because they combine well with both watercolors and inks.

Felt-Tip Pens

Felt-tip pens are useful for quick preliminary or final sketches. Designers often use them for the special effects that the bold strokes of these pens provide. They can be used in preliminary sketches to fill in braids, buttons, shoes, belts, and other accessories quickly. While these pens have other uses, they are expensive and dry out quickly, so they are a marginal investment for the beginning design student.

Papers

For preliminary sketches it is important to use paper that is inexpensive but takes pencil drawing smoothly. As a beginning student it is important to feel you do not have to make a perfect first sketch. Beginning sketches need to be experimental in nature, allowing you to put down many ideas in rough form. Newsprint is too soft, and most watercolor paper is too expensive: however, several companies put out jumbo pads of mixed media paper that serve this purpose. They are about an inch thick, contain about 100 sheets, and take pencil, ink, and watercolor well.

The ideal paper size for costume drawing is 11" × 14". This allows you to place a 12" figure on the paper. Smaller figures tend to be difficult to "read." Many designers choose to do larger sketches, but few do smaller drawings. Some colored papers, such as Canson papers, take watercolor well and offer a wide range of background colors. Mat board also works for this purpose. Colored papers are useful for designers who want to create a specific mood for a play or production with their sketches by use of the background color. If you use colored papers, you need to work with the gouache or casein watercolors, or with acrylics. These paints are thicker and will keep true colors on these backgrounds; transparent watercolors tend to disappear or change color.

When costume designers move from approved preliminary sketches to final sketches, they usually choose from many varieties of watercolor paper. D'Arches hot press 140 weight is one of the most desirable watercolor papers. It is smooth for accurate drawing and takes watercolors exceptionally well. Most watercolor papers come in a 22" × 30" sheet and can be cut to the desired size.

Lightweight watercolor board is also good for final sketches. Heavier watercolor board, although it produces superb color, is very heavy to ship or to carry in your portfolio.

Brushes

Regular watercolor brushes come in a variety of sizes and prices. It is worth the investment to buy one or two good brushes. Most designers need a small brush for detail and a larger brush for rendering large sections. Red sable brushes are very expensive but usually worth the cost. They hold the water better than cheaper brushes and provide a smoother flow of paint. The brushes that come with the Grumbacher Brilliant watercolor set are acceptable. Another choice is the Japanese brush. A #2 or a #3 brush can be used easily for large sections of wash, and the point is useful for details and smaller sections of paint. These brushes are not expensive and are thus easy to replace when they wear out.

Drawing File

Students and designers soon learn the value of a file of pictures and drawings collected from newspaper ads, magazines, catalogues, postcards, or prints. The file can be organized three ways: (1) full male and female bodies, relaxed and active figure poses, arms, legs, feet, faces, hair, shoes, and jewelry; (2) fabric folds and drape and textures such as plaids, prints, satins, furs, velvets, crepes, sequins, and knits; and (3) floors, washes, and backgrounds. You may find other categories helpful. These clippings are enormously useful for finding ideas for different figure poses and fabric textures quickly for your sketches. If you use a light table, you can trace these poses, arm positions, or leg or foot positions onto your paper with ease and flexibility.

Light Table

The light box or light table is a useful tool for designers and students. Although it is possible to hold drawing paper up to a window to quickly recreate ideas on another piece of paper, it is easier to use a light table. Light tables can be purchased or made at home. A 12" × 15" size is adequate for costume sketching.

You can put complete or partial figures together on the light table to create a variety of figure poses quickly and easily on your drawing paper. This helps you get figures down on paper so that you can move on to working on design ideas. You can photocopy these figures to work out many ideas on one original figure. This is a helpful shortcut because the beginning student usually spends a lot of time creating a figure on paper. The time is better spent working on research and costume design ideas to go on the figure.

Chapter *3*

Learning to See Color

Most people think they understand and see color accurately. In fact, very few do. Apples are seldom red. Skin tones are not white or black. We wonder at Monet's paintings of haystacks showing different colors at different times of the day. The colors are from Monet's eye and brain as perceived through light. Learning to see color is more important than understanding color theory. However, both are useful.

Most of us look at color without really seeing differences in value, chroma, or saturation.

Color probably is the design element that first affects the audience. It is emotional, intuitive, and projects the mood of the production. Color has three qualities: hue, value, and saturation. The artistic use of color requires an understanding of each of these elements.

Hue

One of the challenging aspects of working with color is that there are many color systems. Imagine the confusion if each country set a standard for time. Instead, Greenwich Mean Time is established in Greenwich, England. This time standard is used by the entire world. However, color wheels are created separately by each paint and color company. For example, the Munsell and Grumbacher companies each have a color wheel. All color wheels are based on the sequence of color appearing in a prism of light, but each company creates a "pure blue." This and each of the twelve hues on one color circle are slightly different from the hues chosen for the color circles of other companies. There are excellent color circles in Itten's books *The Art of Color* and *The Elements of Color*.

Keep a color wheel with you as you work. Color memory does not exist. While it is possible for a person to reproduce a musical note or a particular shape, even the best colorists cannot match up

a hue from memory. A color swatch is necessary, be it colored paper, fabric, or watercolor. This is due to the fact that a color, the light, and the eye are in continual change.

Color relationships are important tools in creating character relationship charts, a graph that physically places characters in close or distant relationships as they are emotionally in a script. Color plots do the same type of physical relationships with swatches of color to demonstrate the character relationships. Design images and/or a color source for costume designs for a production can be found in a reproduction of a painting. The color palette in a painting can capture the mood desired in the costumes. Color swatches from magazine papers, color aids papers, or fabric swatches are helpful to have in front of you when you are working. A useful color source is a painting that captures the mood and feeling of the play and illuminates the director's concept. The painter has worked out color relationships in the painting. You can match colored papers to this painting reproduction or, with watercolors, paint swatches of the colors to use in a relationship chart.

Hue is also called chroma. It appears in a pure form on the color wheel or color circle. Each step on the color wheel is a change of hue. Most commercial color wheels are twelve hues. The color circle Figure 3.1 is from the book *The Art of Color* by Johannes Itten. Most color circles start with yellow at the top and continue in sequence yellow, yellow/orange, orange, red/orange, red, red/violet, violet, blue/violet, blue, blue/green, green, yellow/green, appearing in the same order as a prism of light or rainbow.

Accordingly, on the color circle complementary colors are those opposite each other. Analogous colors are side by side. Primary colors are red, yellow, and blue. Secondary colors are orange, green, and purple. Intermediary colors are a mixture of a primary and secondary color such as yellow and green.

Value

Value is how light or dark a color appears. The value scale chart from Johannes Itten's book *The Art of Color*, Figure 3.2, shows twelve steps of gray from white to black. This chart also shows the twelve hues of the color wheel in the same twelve value steps from light to dark.

When you view a twelve-step value scale chart, pure hues from the color wheel appear at different placements. A pure yellow is step three on the value scale chart, while purple is a step nine. Red and green are both step six on the value scale and thus create an equal gray in a black and white photograph. Yellow and purple are the extremes of light and dark on a color circle.

Pastels or tints are the top two or three steps of a value scale chart. The lower values are called shades or tones and are the bottom three steps on a value scale chart. Learning to differentiate values is important for theatre designers, as design work in the theatre is often seen at a distance. Distance causes equal values to blend together, as they do at the horizon line. Light/dark contrast is one of the strongest elements in design. Look at Japanese ink paintings or the painter Rembrandt's work for examples. The contrast between light and dark often brings more focus to a costume design than the choice of hue.

Saturation

Saturation is the purity of a color. Only pure hues appear on a color wheel. The opposite of a saturated or pure color is a dull or diluted color. Colors may be diluted four ways using white, black, gray, or the complement. Each of these lowers the purity of a hue and dilutes or dulls the color. A saturated color appears stronger when surrounded by dull or neutral colors. Light/dark contrast will take focus away from saturated colors, so avoid this contrast when emphasizing saturation. The paintings of De la Tour are examples of this saturated/dull contrast.

The two pure hues opposite each other in Figure 3.3 show pure hues graying out and becoming less saturated and lower in value as they are combined with increasing amounts of the complementary color. The equal amounts of the two complements create a neutral color. It is called a chromatic gray because it is a gray/neutral made from two hues (i.e., red and green). This is a form of additive color. Using a complementary hue to lower the value of a color adds color to color.

Subtractive color happens when the value of a hue is lowered with an achromatic neutral. Achromatic neutrals are white, black, or gray (a combination of the black and white). Subtractive color takes away the amount of chroma present in a space. Black, white, and gray do not appear on the color circle or in a prism of light. Whenever you subtract hue from a color, you also reduce the saturation.

Complements

It is important to understand the law of complements to use color artistically. Color is a physiological phenomenon. It appears in the human eye and brain. Two individuals can see the same color differently. So differently, in fact, that some individuals cannot distinguish between what others see as two unique colors. This also explains the condition called color blindness.

As mentioned earlier, every hue has a complement. They are directly opposite each other on the color circle. The law of complements has three rules. Complements used together make each other vivid or strong—for example, the use of red and green as Christmas colors. Second, they annihilate each other when mixed in equal amounts and become a gray neutral. Third, the eye requires the complement of a color and will create it if it is not present.

This phenomenon is called "after image." When you look at a red circle for twenty or thirty seconds and then look at a white sheet of paper, your eye creates a green circle on the paper. This color cannot be photographed. It appears only in the human eye and brain and is caused by the physiological need to create the complementary color. Munsell calls this visual comfort. Indeed, use of color complements is balanced and comfortable to the human eye.

If you look at a single saturated color for a time, without any neutral or other color present, physical discomfort arises. This can cause headaches and will force people to look away from the color for relief. In addition, the eye will slowly build up the complement on the original color or a nearby neutral. For example, a red will slowly display a greenish tint, becoming less saturated. The eye will create a visual color balance wherever an imbalance exists.

Complementary "balance" is a physiological process required by the brain. It is important to recognize that color balance is a psychophysiological phenomenon and not a decorative principle. This use of complementary color balance appears in many paintings in subtle and carefully articulated ways. The paintings of Matisse are good examples.

Complementary relationships are those opposite each other on the color circle and also are established by any square, rectangle, or triangle within the color circle. These double-complements offer a wide choice of complementary relationships, and each can be mixed in a range of values.

Simultaneous Contrast

Simultaneous contrast, so named by Mr. Itten, is the use of complementary colors in an unbalanced way. When an artist like Van Gogh chooses colors that are not balanced as complements but one step off of the complement, this imbalance forces the eye to try to create visual balance. It is an uncomfortable and often vibrating visual effect. The eye does not want to view this color effect for very long. Many Op-Art painters of the 1960s such as Olitski used this principle. Some of the colors appear to vibrate or move as you look at them, as they cause unbalance in the eye. Painters who want an unsettling effect or mood often use an unbalanced color palette. The use of simultaneous contrast creates the opposite effect of complementary colors which, appear visually balanced and can be comfortably viewed for a great length of time.

Warm/Cool Color Usage

To understand the use of warm and cool hues means you must first understand that a color appears warm or cool depending on its neighboring colors. The same color can appear warm as red-violet relative to blue. However, the same red-violet appears cool relative to orange. Thus, having colors appear warm or cool depends on the selection of adjacent colors. The important principle to remember is that color is changeable. Neighboring colors can make a color appear warm or cool, and also lighter or darker. They can even create a change of hue.

Changing Color

Color is the most relative medium in art. It is constantly changing. It changes with neighboring colors, as illustrated here. It also changes with the light source, daylight, artificial light, types of artificial light, the time of day, and how rested or tired are the eyes of the observer.

Colors are also perceived differently when the are in large or small proportions and whether they are near or far away. Impressionist painters used small dots of color to merge into one new color. These can be viewed up close or at a distance to see varying color effects. Figure 3.4, from Josef Albers' book *Interaction of Color*, illustrates how one color can be perceived as two different colors if the neighboring colors are changed.

Color in Light

The preceding study of color is related to color in pigment, dye, or fabrics. Color in light affects all stage design and is based on a different set of primary and secondary colors. An important rule to help you understand color in light is that three primary colors or a pair of complements create white light. This is white light with additive color, and it is important in theatre design to keep colors true at a distance.

Secondly, color in light and color in pigment continue to work on the laws of complements. If a yellow light focuses on a purple dress or set piece, the purple hue will turn gray. This will cause the same effect as mixing equal amounts of two complements in paint.

Summary

In costume design, it is important to realize that value differences, or light-dark contrast, are visually stronger than hue differences. Likewise, saturation contrast, from dull to pure hues, is also visually stronger than most hue differences.

They affect a costume design by making it more interesting to the eye as well as visually stronger at a distance under stage lighting. The artistic use of hue, value, saturation, complements, and simultaneous color relationships can create the mood of a play through color.

Definitions

Encyclopedia: "Color—property of light that depends on wavelengths. Apparent color of object depends on the wavelength of light it reflects. Object that reflects all wavelengths appears white, one that reflects none black."

Johannes Itten: "Colors are forces, radiant energies that affect us positively or negatively, whether we are aware of it or not."

Figure 3.1 Twelve-part color circle, developed from the primary colors yellow/red/blue and the secondary colors orange/green/violet.

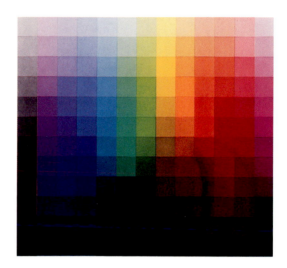

Figure 3.2 Twelve steps of gray from white to black, and the twelve hues of the color circle in matching brilliances.

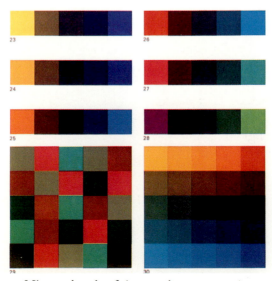

Figure 3.3. Complementary contrast. Mixture bands of six complementary pairs.

Figure 3.4. A color has many faces—the relativity of color 1 color looks like 2.

Chapter *4*

Rendering Fabrics

Satin

Satin is a weave of fabric that is distinguished by a shiny surface. It is usually woven in silk or rayon fibers. It can have various backings from a rib back to a crepe back. Satin is woven in different weights from a stiff, heavier-weight fabric called bridal satin to lighter-weight and beautifully draping creped back satin.

Figure 4.1 Satin.

Velvet

Velvets have a luxurious look because of the depth of pile which creates a soft texture. Called velvet, velveteen, or velours, they are usually woven in cotton, rayon, or silk. The weaving process is like that of carpeting and terry towels where an extra loop is added to the weave, creating a three dimensional fabric. Velveteen is cotton fabric that washes and dyes easily.

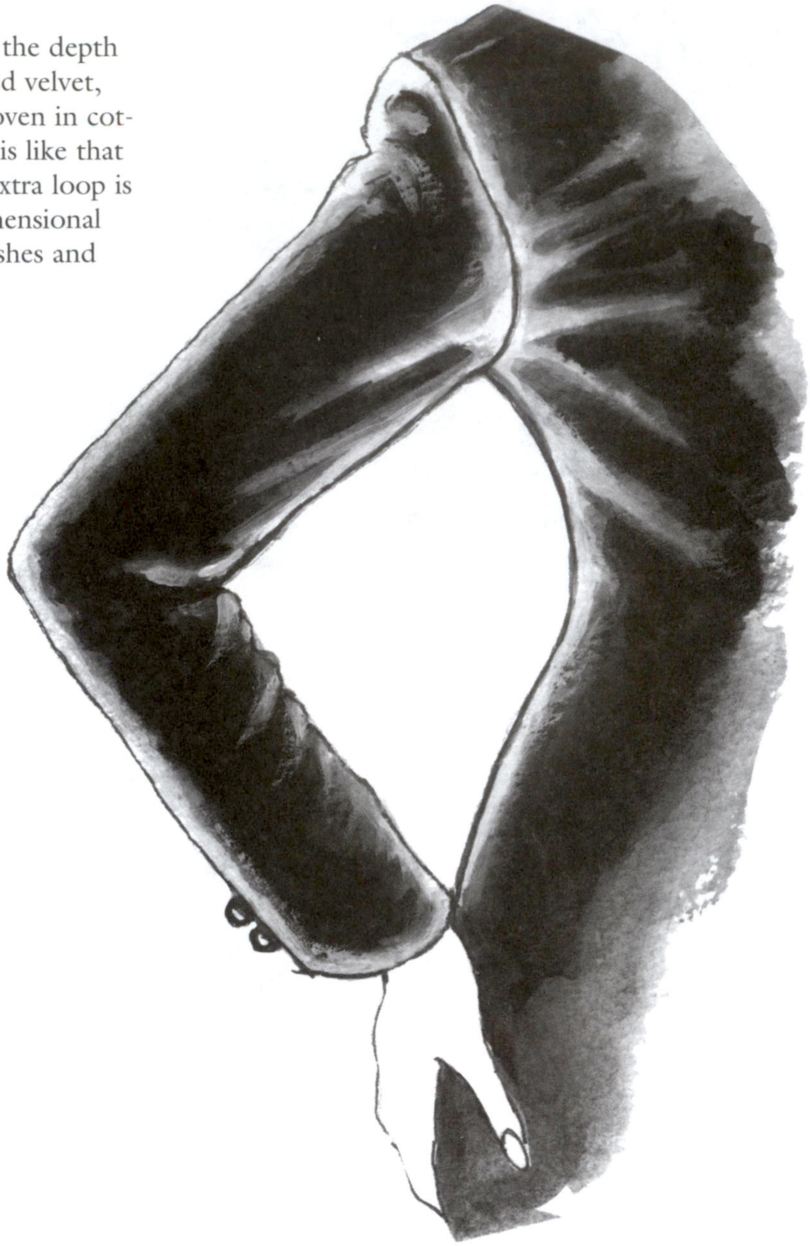

Figure 4.2 Velvet.

Crepe

Textiles woven in a creped weave have a soft and flowing quality. Silk, wool, acetate, or rayon fibers are used predominantly for this weave. Crepes are woven with yarn in a twisted or crinkled state (instead of being stretched flat before weaving). They therefore have a give or stretch and can drape, following the curves of the body.

Figure 4.3 Crepe.

Chiffon

Chiffon is a lightweight, sheer, transparent fabric, as are georgette and organdy. While chiffon and organdy are a plain weave, georgette is a creped weave. Organdy usually has added sizing that gives the fabric stiffness. Transparent fabrics are often woven in rayon and silk, but also in wool, linen, or cotton fibers.

Figure 4.4 Chiffon.

Fur

Fur and leather are not woven textiles, as such, but are animal skins and are interesting to render. Furs vary in texture and color but invariably have thickness, depth, and a range of hues and values in one sample.

Figure 4.5 Fur.

Chapter 5

Computer Aids for Costume Rendering

With the advent of the personal computer, computer-aided rendering of costumes has become increasingly popular. There are now many software packages that lend themselves to costume design and costume drawing. Like all computer programs, the ones discussed here are constantly changing and being updated. New programs appear regularly. Programs such as Adobe Photoshop, Corel Draw 8, Painter 5.5, Poser 3, Adobe Illustrator and Freehand have wide adaptability to costume rendering. Nic Ularu discusses computer drawing for costume design in *Theatre Design and Technology* (summer 1999): "I think of the computer as a tool, an intermediary phase that doesn't replace, but in fact enhances the impression of directness of touch I, and others, value in my renderings."

Two approaches to costume design on the computer are:

1. Drawing on a graphics tablet with a graphics pen and then reworking the drawing on the computer. Working with a graphics tablet and pen, you can choose from a variety of pencil, pen and brush, and airbrush tools. As you draw on the tablet, you can also use the pen to erase as you would with a regular pencil.
2. Scan a costume drawing into the computer and alter or add to the sketch using software programs for drawing and painting. You can delete parts of the drawing or add to it.

Areas to Consider for Computer Rendering Enhancement

1. The Face

After a sketch is scanned into the computer, add a face to the sketch using Adobe Photoshop and a photograph of the actor. Period faces can also be researched and scanned. Alter the face on the sketch to create some of the characteristics desirable in that character or a particular period look. For example, a high forehead distinguishes the 1780s for women. Facial hair such as beards, sideburns, or a moustache might help the 19th-century "look" for the male figure.

2. The Background

Adobe PhotoShop is a useful program for altering backgrounds, to bring a sketch visually forward or to create a mood. The desired effect might be lighter or darker, tragic or comic, or even 18th-century rococo wallpaper. It is also possible to make hues more saturated, or grayer and less saturated. The smudge tool can be used to create a shadow behind a figure or down one side of the page.

These are useful quick effects to try when you scan a pencil sketch and want to look for background effects. It is also possible to scan a clipping for use as a background image. This might include a line drawing of period architecture, furniture, gardens, or an abstraction of the scenic design for the production. There are endless ideas available that help evoke the images desired by the designer and director. They can help place the costume sketch in context.

3. The Pose

If you choose to draw on a graphics tablet, it is possible to change poses quickly. Print or save the sketches and you can add to your work with further research at a later date.

A program called Poser has a wide variety of male, female, and child figures that can be placed in many configurations. This seems to be especially useful for dance choreography, commedia dell'arte characters, or other physically active types such as musical comedy, mime, or clown costume drawings.

4. Color Changes (Hue and Value)

Colors can be made brighter or duller, lighter or darker on individual costume items in a sketch. Make a shirt brighter, a skirt darker, or you can also lighten the whole sketch. One of the most useful and creative tools is the ability to make colors opaque or transparent. This allows for opaque fabric with a transparent overlay or transparent fabric over a silhouette.

5. Lettering

The range of type fonts available on computers offers many styles and sizes of lettering for completing your sketch. Pick a font that goes with the style of the sketch, or style of period or production. Use a computer font to add the title of the play, character, act, scene, date, location of production, or the designer's name. You can select the size and style of lettering to suit the proportion and mood of the sketch.

6. Special Effects

It is possible to eliminate parts of a photograph or sketch using tools called smudge and burn. Take out a background. Eliminate a person or character. Add snow, smoke, or other effects.

7. Makeup

Scan a photo of an actor and then use the tablet to draw the character makeup you desire. Create an old-age or middle-age look. Animals, masks, and monsters can be adapted with line and color. Figure 5.1 shows an actor's face and a drawing for a wolf makeup done over the original face. The actor is Steve Bauer. The wolf makeup design was created digitally by Marianne Wittelsberger of Jokesters® Productions, an Award Winning Entertainment Company based in Hollywood, CA, which she owns and operates with her partner, Steve Bauer.

8. Personalizing Your Sketch

After printing sketches worked or reworked on the computer, personalize costume sketches with pencil or pen detailing. This might include details and finishing touches on lace, braid, buttons, or specific shoe or hat trimmings. You can go back to the sketch with a wash of permanent India ink to create a feeling of depth or a more three-dimensional effect on the sketch. Strong highlights can be added to a sketch with a thick or opaque mixture of white gouache or casein watercolor. Pick a direction for your light source, such as left to right, and use this direction consistently in all of your costume sketches for a production.

Watercolors, pencil, colored pencils, watercolor pencils, pastels, inks can be used to make background effects on a sketch. Add or select fabric swatches as early as possible in the design process. They complete the images in the sketch and give you, as the designer, a sense of the flow of the fabric. Keep the swatches in the same proportion as their use in the costume—smaller swatches for trim colors, larger swatches for major garments.

Steve Bauer

Step 1. Scan the headshot of the actor into PhotoShop and save to your hard drive as a PhotoShop file. This will allow you to design the makeup in layers and to make changes to the design. The headshot will become the background layer.

Steve Bauer

Step 2. On a new layer, begin your design with the base makeup color using any of the paint tools, such as the airbrush, paintbrush, or pencil. Marianne used the airbrush and set the opacity to 74% to allow some of the actor's features to show through.

Steve Bauer

Step 3. On separate layers create highlights and shadows with the paint tools. Marianne used the airbrush in different sizes and colors along with the smudge tool to create the desired design. Using different layers allowed Marianne to experiment with a variety of effects.

Steve Bauer

Step 4. On the top layer she created the costume headdress the actor would be wearing to complete the wolf makeup. Creating designs digitally adds to the flexibility and convenience of a designer. Completed designs can be emailed to the production team and changes can be made quickly.

Figure 5.1. Steve Bauer in wolf makeup. (©1999 Marianne Wittelsberger Jokesters® Productions)

Chapter 6

Creating a Period Silhouette
3000 B.C.–1969 A.D.

Egyptian

3100–30 B.C.

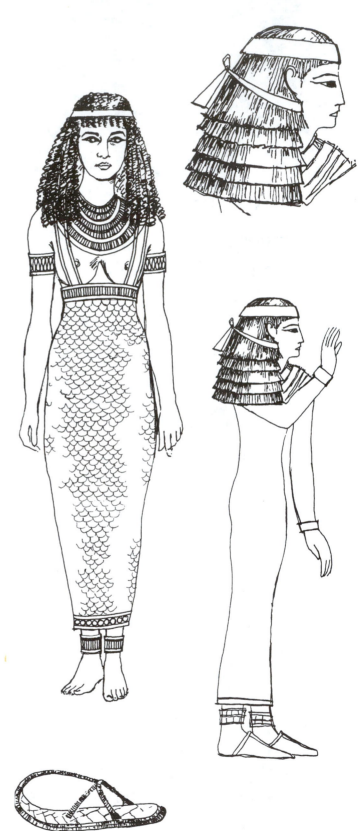

Headdress/Hair

Women wear elaborate wigs in varying lengths, some reaching just above the waist. They are decorated with gold bands and beads and are braided or curled into tight spirals. The wig covers a shaved head. Headbands have insignias on the front, such as the lotus bud, asp, cobra, sun disk, rosette, or papyrus. The gold vulture headdress resembles the wings and head of a vulture. Decorative striped fabric may cover the wig. Women frequently wear large loop or disk earrings. Some women have perfumed oil cones on top of their wigs.

Neck/Shoulder/Arm

A wide collar encircles the neck from shoulder to shoulder. Made of gold beads, clay beads, jeweled stones, or enamelware, the collar accompanies all garments. The upper and lower arms are frequently adorned with wide matching bracelets. The shoulder may be covered by a short pleated cape or by a longer robe that is pleated in over the shoulder and upper arm. The kalasiris, a straight, unbelted, fitted sheath, has wide straps that extend from under the bustline over the shoulder.

Waist/Hip/Skirt

The robe pleats in and belts at the waist. The kalasiris ends at midcalf. A pleated skirt may be worn with the cape; it falls from waist to ankle. Robes or skirts may be sheer, revealing part of the body underneath. Belts may be jeweled, and ankle bracelets may match the armbands. Bleached white linen is the common fabric for robes and skirts. The kalasiris is often multipatterned in bright colors.

Footwear

Egyptians go barefoot or wear sandals of reed or leather. The thong sandal and the toe sandal are popular styles.

Egyptian

3100–30 B.C.

Headdress/Hair

In the Egyptian culture wigs are a major part of dress. Elaborate wigs of human or horse hair are braided into lengths sometimes reaching halfway down the chest or the back. These wigs often have gold bands or beads braided into them. They are usually black and worn with many styles of headdress. One of these, the vulture headdress, is made of gold and fits the head like a cap.

Fillet headbands are made of gold or silver and are inlaid with stones. Many of the circlet bands have a motif on the front, such as the lotus bud, cobra, sun disk, asp, papyrus, or rosettes. Striped linen headdresses, called wig covers, are worn over wigs. Several types of war helmets and crowns are used. Shaved heads are visible when wigs are removed indoors.

Neck/Shoulder/Arm

A wide collar adorns the neckline from shoulder to shoulder. Collars made of gold, jewels, beads, and enamelware accompany all garments. They are tapered to fit smoothly around the neck. Matching armbands and wristbands appear on the upper and lower arm. The shoulder line is natural. The tunic is a T-shaped garment with a round neck and short sleeves. Other garments, such as the robe or the shawl, are pleated in across the shoulders and upper arm. The robe is pulled in at the waist by a belt.

Waist/Hip/Skirt

The schenti, or loincloth, is pleated around the body from the waist to the knee. Some schentis have a starched and decorated triangular piece on the front called an apron. The skirt wraps or drapes on the body and extends from the waist to the ankle. Longer garments, such as the robe, wrap to the front of the body and fasten with a wide, jeweled belt at the waist. Garments may be layered one over the other, such as a tunic over a loincloth or a robe over a schenti. Ankle bracelets may match the armbands and wristbands.

Footwear

Men wear reed or leather sandals in several styles. The toe thong with a wide strap across the instep is a favorite style. Many Egyptians go barefoot.

33

Biblical (Assyrian, Persian, Hebrew)

1250–333 B.C.

Headdress/Hair

Very few sources for female hair or clothing are available for any of these groups. Assyrian and Persian women have tightly curled hair combed into stylized patterns. Most hairstyles are shoulder-length and combed straight back behind the ears. Hair can be pulled into a chignon or bun at the back of the neck. Headdress consists of a diadem, or a wide headband, of metal or cloth. Shawls may be draped over the head for protection from the sun. Assyrian and Persian women wear large earrings.

Neck/Shoulder/Arm

The neckline is round, and the shoulder is soft. Women wear a long tunic with short or long sleeves. Drapes or stoles are worn over any tunics. Assyrian women wear shawls with heavy, thick woolen fringe on the edges. Both Persian and Assyrian tunics may have overall geometric patterning in colors. The Hebrew costume is usually of solid colors or woven stripes. Sleeves are straight in Assyrian robes, and straight or bell-shaped in Persian and Hebrew robes. Persian and Assyrian women wear gold or iron necklaces and bracelets.

Waist/Hip/Skirt

The waistline is belted on most tunics. Hebrews sometimes wear a straight, unbelted, narrow tunic. The tunic is ankle-length and narrow to moderately full. Hems are decorated with geometric patterns. Assyrian tunics usually have heavy woolen fringe, almost like tassels, on the bottom.

Footwear

Assyrian footwear consists of sandals of various types. The wedge-heel shape is popular. Persians wear a soft leather slip-on shoe. Hebrews usually wear slippers.

Biblical (Assyrian, Persian, Hebrew)

1250–333 B. C.

Headdress/Hair

Most hairstyles are shoulder-length and are accompanied by full beards. Both Assyrian and Persian men have dark, tightly curled hair and beards. The Assyrian beard is square, and the Persian beard is more pointed. Hebrew hairstyles and beards are natural, full, and untrimmed. Assyrian and Persian males wear large bold earrings.

Assyrian male headdress consists primarily of felt hats shaped like a fez, 6" to 8" high, and sloping in slightly from the head to the crown. Persian felt hats frequently flare out from the head and are slightly taller. The Hebrew headdress is a large chest-length scarf held on by a headband. All three groups wear wide headbands. Assyrian and Persian headbands are often heavily ornamented. Assorted helmets are worn for warfare.

Neck/Shoulder/Arm

A long tunic is the basis for most clothing. The neckline is round, and the shoulder line is natural. Assyrians wear fitted short-sleeved tunics with large heavily fringed shawls wrapped over them. The shawls pass over one shoulder and under the opposite arm. The Persian robe has a full, flared sleeve that comes to the wrist. Hebrew robes can have a narrow sleeve like that of a caftan or a bell sleeve. A rectangular robe that opens in the front is called an aba. Heavy iron bracelets may be worn at the wrist.

Hip/Waist/Skirt

Most tunics and robes are ankle-length and belted at the waist. Persians wear bracchae, a trouser cut full at the waist and hip and narrow on the lower leg. They also wear stockings. Most Assyrian tunics have a 4" to 6" length of thick fringe on the bottom. Both Assyrians and Persians use overall patterning. Hebrews use woven stripes on many garments.

Footwear

Assyrians wear a wedge-heel sandal. Persians wear a pointed-toe boot for horseback riding, and other ankle-high boots and slippers. Hebrews prefer a soft slipper with a rounded toe.

Archaic Greek

800–480 B.C.

Headdress/Hair

Tightly curled and wavy hair appears on the forehead, where it is sometimes styled, and in long
strands halfway down the chest. A fillet headband
supports the hair. Women wear a diadem called a
stephanie on the front of the head. It is sometimes
combined with a veil.

Neck/Shoulder/Arm

Doric or Ionic chitons start at the shoulder, leaving
the arms bare, or pleat down the arms to create a
sleeve effect. Chitons are created from rectangular
pieces of fabric. A round neckline is shaped by the
drape of the chiton. The shoulder line is soft and
natural. The Doric chiton has an overfold of fabric
hanging freely from the shoulder. The chiton is
pinned with small decorative safety pins called fibulae or sewn at the shoulder. A Doric chiton may be
layered over an Ionic chiton to create an effect popular among Greek women. The himation, a rectangular shawl, may be worn over the shoulders or
wrapped around the body over the chiton.

Waist/Hip/Leg

A belt at the waist of the chiton can be used to create blousing above the belt. Chitons vary from slender to fairly full and are ankle-length. Woven border
patterns appear on the edges of chitons, and in the
Archaic period most chitons have a woven overall
pattern in colors. Chitons, made of crinkly wool,
develop draped styles during the Archaic period that
carry over into the complex and beautiful draping
of the Classic Greek costume.

Footwear

Women go barefoot or wear leather sandals.

Archaic Greek

800–480 B.C.

Headdress/Hair

The long, curly hair of the Archaic period is distinctly different from the short Classic style. The dark, tightly waved hair is generally shoulder-length and rolled about the head. Beards are curly and rounded or pointed. The most common headwear is the fillet headband. Travelers wear the petasos, a felt or straw sun hat. The Phrygian cap, a type of wool stocking cap, appears for the first time. High-crested helmets with nose guards are part of combat dress.

Neck/Shoulder/Arm

The major garments of the Archaic period have the same names as garments from the Classic period, but the look is very different. The chiton is a rectangle of fabric, pinned at the shoulders and belted at the waist, in a wavy, crinkly wool. It drapes softly at the neck and shoulder, and it pins at the shoulder with a fibula. The chiton could also be sewn at the shoulder. The fabric folds on one side of the body.

The himation and the chlamys are drapes that may be worn by themselves or over a chiton. The himation is a large rectangle wrapped around the body. The chlamys is a shorter square cape pinned at the neck or shoulder Archaic chitons frequently have overall patterning and woven borders in one or more colors. The Ionic chiton falls straight from shoulder to hem. The Doric chiton has an overfold of fabric falling from the shoulder to the waist. A breastplate, called a lorica, is worn over a chiton for military dress.

Waist/Hip/Leg

The chiton belts at the waist and blouses softly above. Border patterns appear on hems and other edges of garments. Geometric patterns may appear over entire garments. Chiton lengths range from the lower hip to the ankle.

Footwear

Men wear several styles of sandals and also go barefoot. Travel and military dress includes midcalf boots that lace up the front and have open toes.

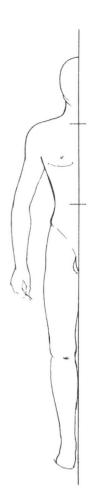

Classic Greek

480 B.C.–A.D. 146

Headdress/Hair

The Classic hairstyle made famous by Greek women consists of softly waved hair, parted in the center and pulled back into a chignon or bun. A headband or a stephanie headdress can be worn with this hairstyle. The stephanie may curve to a point in the front, giving it a tiara shape. It is usually made of gold. A soft cap or a scarf sometimes adorns the head. Gold earrings are worn. Makeup is not used.

Neck/Shoulder/Arm

The neck and shoulder line are soft and natural. The chiton, a large rectangle of fabric, is draped and pinned on the body to form the major garment. It is pinned across the shoulders with small decorative safety pins called fibulae. The chiton may be narrow and end at the shoulder, elbow, or wrist. The neckline consists of a soft, curved drape. The chiton is made of a lightweight wool that pleats in to drape gracefully on the arm. The Ionic chiton is a length of fabric reaching from shoulder to ankle. The Doric chiton has an overfold of fabric that folds down to form a separate piece of fabric hanging freely from the shoulder. If a himation, a rectangular overgarment, is worn, it wraps over one shoulder and around the body.

Waist/Hip/Hem

The waist of the chiton is belted in and bloused softly over the belting. A special blousing at the waist, created by double belting, is called a kolpos. Chitons are sometimes layered with an Ionic chiton, or more slender chiton, underneath, and a Doric chiton, or fuller chiton, over the top. Most chitons worn by women reach the ankle or the top of the foot.

Footwear

A slender sandal, wrapped above or below the ankle, is worn. Women also go barefoot.

Classic Greek

480 B.C.–A.D. 146

Headdress/Hair

Hair is short and layered in the Classic period. Most men are clean-shaven, but older men may wear full beards. Headdress consists of the fillet headband and the petasos, a sun hat of straw or felt. Crested helmets accompany military wear.

Neck/Shoulder/Arm

The major Greek garment, the chiton, is a rectangle of fabric pleated and draped on the body. The pleats gather in and are held in place by a fibula, a safety pin with a decorative brooch on the top. The shoulder is soft, and the neckline has a soft drape at the center front and center back. There is a fold of fabric on one side of the body, and there are two selvages on the other. The chiton may fasten at the shoulder and leave the arms bare, or it may be symmetrically pleated down the arm to the elbow or the wrist. The Ionic chiton hangs straight from shoulder to ankle.

The chlamys, a short cape, fastens on one shoulder. Other drapes, such as the himation, are complete garments by themselves or are worn over a chiton. They wrap around the body, usually over one shoulder and under the other arm. A kolpos, a special type of blousing at the waist, is created by double-belting.

Waist/Hip/Leg

The chiton is belted and bloused so that part of the fabric hangs with a fullness above the waist. Beautiful blousing and draping is one of the secrets of the look of Classic Greek garments. The chiton ends at midthigh, knee, or ankle. Chitons may be layered one over another, which creates additional fullness. Underchitons are often opaque, and overchitons are made of transparent fabrics.

Footwear

Bare feet or sandals complement the Greek belief in the beautiful body and in graceful movement. Sandals are low or may lace above the ankle. Military wear is a calf-high boot called a buskin.

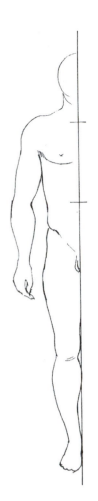

Roman

753 B.C.–A.D. 476

Headdress/Hair

The hair of Roman women goes from softly waved chignons and braids to complex curls and artificial hair in the later periods. Some of the later styles achieve great height at the front of the head. Roman matrons wear elaborate makeup and jewelry. The lips may be tinted and eyebrows darkened. Long or loop gold earrings are popular and hair ornaments also are beautifully done. The flammeum, or veil, is the major headdress and is usually worn with a stephanie or a tiara-shaped headband.

Neck/Shoulder/Arm

The major garment is a rectangle of fabric called a stola which drapes with fibulae down the arm to about the elbow. An overdrape called a palla is frequently wrapped over the left shoulder and around the body. It may be pulled over the head to form a type of hood. Bracelets of gold are worn with the earrings and hair ornaments. Clavi, vertical bands of decorated fabric or embroidery, go from shoulder to hem.

Waist/Hip/Skirt

The waist of the stola is belted and softly bloused. The stola is moderately full and reaches to the ankle or top of the foot. The overdrape usually wraps around the hip of the body and over the left arm.

Footwear

Sandals have light- or medium-weight soles. They may lace in the front or around the ankle.

Roman

753 B.C.–A.D. 476

Headdress/Hair

Most Roman men wear a feathered or layered hair-cut with bangs on the forehead. It is cut short at the nape of the neck. Philosophers wear beards, but most males are clean shaven. The only headwear are helmets worn by the military, a straw hat or petasos worn by workers, and a hooded poncho worn by travelers. The emperor wears a laurel wreath. The fullness of the toga can be pulled over the head to create a hood effect and is used for mourning.

Neck/Shoulder/Arm

The tunica, a straight T-shaped garment with round neckline and natural shoulder line, is the primary garment worn by all males. It can have short or wrist-length sleeves. A short-sleeved tunica is frequently worn over a long-sleeved one.

Overgarments, such as the toga or pallium, can be worn over the tunica. The toga comes in many forms, each with a specific meaning. One must be awarded the right to wear a toga. The toga usually drapes over the left shoulder, leaving the right arm free. The pallium may be worn by itself. Military officers wear a lorica or breastplate, over a tunica. It has strips of leather at the shoulders and hips called lapits.

Waist/Hip/Leg

The tunica is belted at the waist and often decorated with clavi, colored vertical bands of fabric going from shoulder to hem. The hem reaches above the knee or just above the ankle.

Footwear

Sandals and boots come in many styles. They vary from a thin dress sandal to a sturdy sandal much like a low-cut shoe. Boots, called caligula, lace up the front and may have ornamental cuffs at the top. Legs are bare but boots come to the midcalf.

Byzantine

324–1453

Headdress/Hair

The hair has a formal look and is rolled up on the sides and into a chignon or bun at the back or the top of the head. Jeweled crowns, tiaras, or circlet headbands and a flammeum, or veil, cover most of the hair. Long drop earrings of pearl or precious stones frame the face.

Neck/Shoulder/Arm

Wide collars or bands of jewels, pearl, and gold cover round necklines. A white inner tunica may show at the wrist, neck, or hem. The outer tunica is made of heavy silk and has a soft shoulder line and a straight or flared sleeve. An embroidered or jeweled band at the wrist may match the decoration at the neckline. Embroidered circles or rectangles may appear on the shoulder. The shoulder is frequently covered by a pallium, a rectangular shawl draped over the right shoulder and down around the left side of the body, or by a cope, a half-circle cape.

Waist/Hip/Skirt

The heavy silk tunica hangs straight or is belted. Clavi, vertical decorated or embroidered panels, may go down the side front and side back of the tunica. Square or round embroidered panels, called segmentae, may appear above the hem of the tunica and on the pallium. Hems reach to the floor and are straight or slightly flared. Hose cover the legs.

Footwear

Embroidered or jeweled cloth or leather slippers show beneath the hem of the tunica. They have round toes and a flat heel.

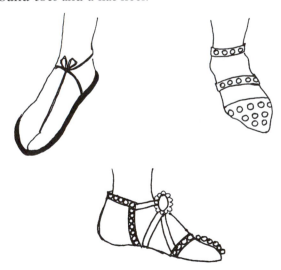

Byzantine

324–1453

Headdress/Hair

The distinctive hairstyle of the Byzantine man, a pageboy, is cut ear-length and curled under in a soft roll. It has a formality that matches the rest of the costume. Neatly trimmed beards and mustaches appear in the latter part of the period. The emperor wears elaborate crowns with large jewels and strands of pearls hanging vertically. The Phrygian cap, a soft stocking-type cap, reappears from the Archaic Greek period. The petasos, or sun hat, and hood provide protection for the common man.

Neck/Shoulder/Arm

The major garment is a knee- or ankle-length tunica with a round neckline. The shoulder line is soft and often decorated with segmentae, embroidered square or round pieces, on one or both shoulders. A straight sleeve extends to the wrist and has embroidered borders. Usually made of heavy silk, the tunica is often embroidered over all. The mantle, a half-circle cape also called a cope, fastens on the right shoulder with a large brooch of pearls and other jewels.

Waist/Hip/Breeches

The tunica belts at the waist or hangs straight. Because the fabrics are stiff silk samites or brocades, there is little drape or blousing to the tunica. Bracchae, which are fitted trousers, or hose cover the legs. A tablion, a rectangular embroidered piece of fabric, attaches to the front and back opening of the cape at waist height. It is a symbol of aristocracy.

Footwear

Shoes are soft slippers in bright colors, often embroidered or jeweled. They come to the ankle or have a strap across the instep and fit low on the foot. Cloth or leather boots are calf-length.

Romanesque

900–1200

Headdress/Hair

Braided hair is long, hanging to the knee, or pulled up and circled into a thick bun at the side of the head. Circlet or fillet headbands are common. A barbette, a linen band, passes from under the chin around the top of the head. The gorget is a piece of cloth tied to cover the neck. It is frequently worn with a wimple, a veil or scarf that covers the head and falls down over the shoulders.

Neck/Shoulder/Arm

The bliaut is a tunic with soft shoulders and a round or keyhole neck. The sleeves may be fitted or bell-shaped, flared below the elbow and are often turned back to form a cuff. Sleeves are cut in one piece with the garment. The bliaut falls from shoulder to ankle or floor. The neckline opening may be laced to close. Colored embroidery in wide bands completes neckline and sleeve edges.

Waist/Hip/Skirt

The bliaut frequently laces up the center back or on the side to give the silhouette a fitted torso and waist. The bliaut may be unbelted or blouse slightly at the waist after belting on the hip. Although the top of the bliaut is fitted, the skirt flares below the hip to create half- to full-circle fullness from hip to floor. A white cotton or linen chemise serves as a slip underneath the bliaut. It also laces shut. These garments are made in two pieces, with a shoulder seam and a side seam. Wide bands of embroidery often decorate the hemline.

Footwear

Women wear cotton or wool stockings. Round-toed shoes with flat soles rise to below the ankle and lace or buckle. Pattens, wooden clogs that slip on over the shoe or hose, are practical for muddy streets and damp cobblestones.

Romanesque

900–1200

Headdress/Hair

Hair is ear- to shoulder-length and unstyled, usually accompanied by a beard and mustache. The hood, a common form of headwear, sometimes has a skirt attached that falls over the shoulders. The point of the hood, called a liripipe, extends down the back, sometimes reaching to the knee. As a fashion statement the liripipe can go across the chest, pass over the shoulder, or even wind around the head. A circlet or fillet headband is both decorative and functional. A coif is a fitted cap that ties under the chin.

Neck/Shoulder/Arm

The bliaut, worn by men and women, is a tunic with a round or keyhole neckline and soft shoulders. The dolman sleeve is cut fuller at the shoulder and narrows as it tapers to the wrist. The bell-shaped sleeve fits at the shoulder and flares widely below the elbow. The hem of the sleeve sometimes turned back to form a cuff.

   Both neckline and wrist may be decorated with 2"- to 3"-wide colored braid. Cloaks or mantles, full- or half-circle, fasten with a brooch at the center neck or at one side on the shoulder. The bliaut often laces at the slit at the neck; it may also lace up the center back or under the arm to create a more fitted torso. A chemise, an undergarment of cotton or linen, is also cut in the shape of a tunic.

Waist/Hip/Skirt

The waistline belts low, at the top of the hip, and the bliaut blouses slightly over the belt. The skirt of the bliaut hangs to knee- or ankle-length, often with a border of braid. A wide belt of leather or cloth may hold a broadsword. The hem of the bliaut is frequently uneven because of the bias drape of the quarter- to half-circle cut of the skirt. Loose trousers called bracchae are often paired with the bliaut. Cross-lacing frequently holds the breeches tighter on the lower leg. Cloaks are knee- or floor-length. Cotton or wool hose are cut to fit the leg. Knitted fabric is also becoming available during this period. Hose tie onto a belt at the waist under the bliaut.

Footwear

Shoes or slippers have round toes and flat soles, and they lace at the front or on the side to just below the ankle. Wooden clogs called pattens slip over shoes to raise them out of the mud.

Early Gothic

1200–1325

Headdress/Hair

Married women wear their hair up in braids circled at the side of the head. Unmarried women may wear their hair down. The gorget and wimple are important in this period. The gorget is a piece of fabric that covers the neck and even the sides of the head. It is paired with the wimple, a veil that covers the top of the head and falls down below the shoulders. The wimple may be held in place with a headband or circlet. The toque is a hat, 2" or 3" high with a slight flare, that can be worn by itself or in combination with a gorget or coif. The coif is a skullcap that ties under the chin.

Neck/Shoulder/Arm

The neckline is soft and round on the cote, a princess-line gown reaching from neck to hem with only side seams. The sleeves fit smoothly and go to the wrist. The cote usually laces up the center back. A full-circle mantle, or cloak, reaches the floor. Braid is usually the only trimming used. It goes around the hems and edges of the cote or mantle.

Waist/Hip/Skirt

The waistline drops, and the cote belts low on the hip. The gown is narrow through the hip and flares into a full skirt that reaches the ankle or the floor. Cotton or wool hose cover the legs and tie onto a belt at the waist.

Footwear

A pointed-toe slipper of leather or cloth with a flat sole or a thin heel is the universal footwear. It comes up to the instep of the foot and may lace on the side. Wooden pattens are worn outdoors with the shoes.

Early Gothic

1200–1325

Headdress/Hair

Men's hair is ear- to shoulder-length and is parted at the center or side. Beards and mustaches are common in this period. The coif, a fitted skullcap, ties under the chin. The coif is also worn under other felt or woolen hats. The hood buttons in the front and has a short skirt covering the shoulders and a small point on the top. The point, called a liripipe, becomes longer later in the period.

Neck/Shoulder/Arm

A round-neck robe called a cote has a soft shoulder and a semifitted sleeve to the wrist. Surcotes, the tabard or cyclas, are worn over the cote. The tabard, a sandwich-board shape, is open at the sides, and has a seam at the shoulder. It is hip-length. The cyclas is sleeveless, has shoulder and side seams, and is usually knee-length. A full-circle mantle or cloak, worn for warmth or outerwear, reaches from the shoulder to the floor.

Waist/Hip/Skirt

Both the cotes and the surcotes belt at the normal waistline. The robes are knee- or ankle-length and semifull in width. They are made of heavy or coarse wool, or of linen. Wool or cotton hose cover the legs.

Footwear

A soft shoe of leather or fabric with a flat heel and a small pointed toe is worn. It usually laces or buttons on the front or side.

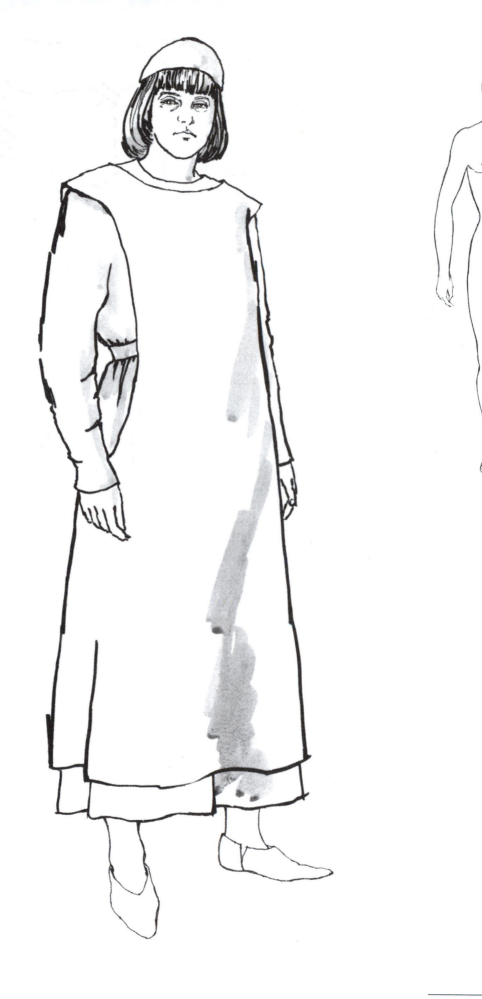

Middle Gothic

1325–1425

Headdress/Hair
Hair rarely shows because it is braided at the side of the head and covered with a mesh cap called a caul or a crespinette. These are made of gold or silver net and may have pearls or jewels as decoration. The headdress is often combined with a roundel or an escoffion, both of which are padded headdresses that give additional height to the head, and a veil, called a wimple.

Neck/Shoulder/Arm
The neck is frequently covered by a gorget, a piece of fabric draped to fasten in back. The first major female garment is the cote, or gown. The second is the sideless gown, a surcote, with a round neckline and a soft shoulder line. The third is the houppelande, which may have a high-standing collar and full bell-shaped sleeves dropping to the floor. It is belted at the waist and opens up the front The cote has a fitted sleeve. The sideless gown is cut open from shoulder to hip like a large jumper.

Waist/Hip/Skirt
The waistline drops to the top of the hip. Most gowns are cut in a princess line without a waistline seam and are belted low on the hip. The sideless gown is open on the sides with a T-shaped piece at the top and a full skirt starting at the hip. If the top piece is made of fur, it is called a plastron. Most skirts of the princess-line gowns are cut narrow at the hips and full at the hem. Gowns start to have a small train at the back of the skirt during this period.

Footwear
Hose cover the legs, and pointed-toe shoes called poulaines are worn. The poulaine has a flat heel, reaches up to the ankle, and usually laces on the side. It is combined with wooden clogs called pattens to protect the shoes and the skirt from damp floors and unpaved streets.

Middle Gothic

1325–1425

Headdress/Hair

Hair length is just below the ears, and headdress is part of fashionable dress in- or outdoors. The coif, a fitted cap that ties under the chin, can be worn alone or with a roundel or chaperon. The roundel is a padded circle of fabric. The chaperon is a roundel with a large drape of fabric worn to one side of the head. It frequently has a long tail of fabric, called a liripipe, worn over one shoulder. The chaperon, made of rich fabrics such as velvet or brocade, often has edges that are cut into petal or scallop shapes called dagging. The turban is popular, and the hood has a liripipe and a skirt that covers the shoulders. Peaked felt hats are worn for hunting.

Neck/Shoulder/Arm

The major garment of this period is the houppelande, a long or knee-length robe that opens up the front. The collar is high around the neck and curved. The shoulders are square, and the bell-shaped sleeves with scallop or leaf-shaped dagged edges reach to the floor. Both sleeves and robe have cartridge pleats, which are vertical pleats that accommodate thick fabrics. These pleats are also called organ-pipe folds. Other cotes and surcotes from the early gothic continue to be worn.

Waist Hip/Hose

The houppelande belts at the waist with a wide, decorative belt. The robe opens in the front showing the legs and wool, cotton, or silk hose. The houppelande reaches to the floor in the front and has a short train in the back. The bastard houppelande is a knee-length version.

Footwear

The long pointed shoe called a poulaine is an ankle-high boot with toes stiffened to reach out in front of the foot. Throughout the period, wooden clogs called pattens slip over the shoes to protect them from muddy streets and ground.

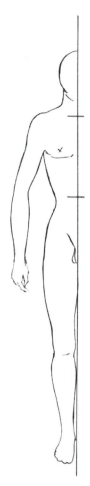

Late Gothic

1425–1485

Headdress/Hair

Women's hair barely shows because it is worn under the tall hennin headdress. The hair on the forehead and at the sides of the face and even the eyebrows is plucked to give a smooth look. The hennin comes in various forms: steeple, butterfly, and heart-shaped. The steeple or cone shape can reach approximately 18" to 30" high. The hennins have sheer veils pinned to them in starched butterfly shapes or in soft drapes that extend around the shoulders. The taller styles are limited to France and Burgundy. The Italians allow hair to show, and the softer roundel, a padded roll, is more popular.

Neck/Shoulder/Arm

A wide V-shaped neckline predominates on the late Gothic gown. The tapered collar goes from the shoulder to the belt at the raised waistline. Sleeves are generally fitted from shoulder to wrist and have a deep cuff that can turn down to cover most of the hand except for the fingertips. Necklaces almost always fill in the neckline.

Waist/Hip/Skirt

The skirt is long, gored, and flowing with a train that can extend 8' to 10' at the back of the skirt and even 2' to 3' on the floor in front. This requires women to lift the front of the skirt to walk. The skirt is narrower at the hips and very full at the hem.

Footwear

Stockings and flat-heeled shoes with long pointed toes barely show until the woman lifts her long skirt to walk. Wooden clogs called pattens slip over the shoes to protect them from cold floors and muddy ground.

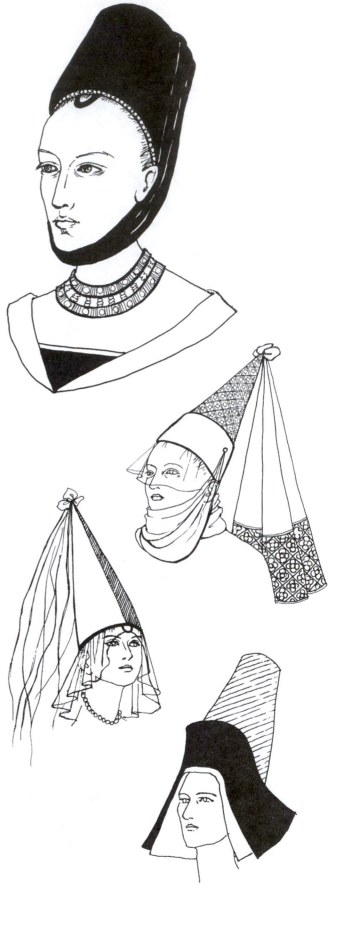

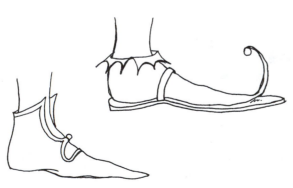

Late Gothic

1425–1485

Headdress/Hair

Hairstyles vary from shoulder-length in the early Gothic period to ear-length and the nape of the neck in the Late Gothic period. The hairline is sometimes shaved at the sides and back of the neck. As the hair gets shorter, the hats get taller. A tall felt hat, called the sugarloaf or steeple hat, matches the tall hennins worn by women. It reaches 8" to 18" in height and includes a jewel or feather for decoration. A padded roll, called a roundel, is popular, as is the chaperon, which is a roundel with an extra drape of fabric tossed to one side of the hat. Many other shapes of felt hats appear as well.

Neck/Shoulder/Arm

Many garments from the Early and Middle Gothic continue to be worn in this period. The predominant male fashion is a new style of doublet called a pourpoint. It has wide shoulders, a tall neckband collar, and sleeves puffed at the shoulder and tapering to the wrist. The front and back have cartridge pleats, which are deep vertical folds that are also called organ-pipe folds. Heavy brocade or velvet fabrics with fur linings add depth to the cartridge pleating.

Waist/Hip/Hose

The waistline of the doublet is low, at the top of the hips, and the cartridge pleats continue into a short peplum reaching the top of the thigh. Joined, fitted hose cover the legs. Separate hose tie onto a belt under the doublet.

Footwear

The most extreme pointed-toe shoes appear in this period. The long points maintain their shape with stiffening in the toe, and they sometimes curve upward. The shoes, called poulaines, are ankle-length. Shoes often slip into wooden pattens, raised clogs with a strap across the instep, for outdoor wear.

Early Renaissance (Italian)

1485–1520

Headdress/Hair

Young women wear their hair long until marriage. Then hair is arranged up in a variety of styles with a chignon at the back and soft curls around the face. Blond hair is fashionable; hair is bleached and fringed into many styles. Headdress includes the small, round Juliet cap, which is worn on the back of the head. Other styles include the coif, the snood (a large hairnet), and a small headband that ties across the forehead.

Neck/Shoulder/Arm

The Early Renaissance gown has a round or rectangular neckline and soft shoulder. Upper and lower sleeves tie into the bodice with laces called points, and the chemise blouses through at the shoulder and elbow in soft puffs. Other sleeves are soft and puffed and extend from shoulder to wrist, and their center front slash reveals an inner lining of a contrasting color. A canvas busk supports the bustline. The chemise is an undergarment, like a slip, that shows at the neckline and through the sections of the sleeves.

Waist/Hip/Skirt

The waist is raised to about halfway between the bustline and the natural waistline. The skirt pleats in to moderate fullness and falls over petticoats and often a small hip roll. The skirt reaches to the floor or the top of the shoe.

Footwear

Stockings are silk or cotton. Most shoes are flat-heeled slippers of velvet or leather. Shoes lace or have a strap across the front.

Early Renaissance (Italian)

1485–1520

Headdress/Hair
Shoulder-length hair is layered into natural waves around the face. Fringed bangs are popular, and most men are clean-shaven. Varieties of shaped felt and velvet hats have jeweled brooches and feathers on the front or side. They are fashionable indoors and outdoors.

Neck/Shoulder/Arm
The chemise shirt gathers into a round neckline or neckband and has full sleeves. The shirt is white cotton or silk and shows at the front of the doublet and where the upper and lower sleeves tie together. The doublet is worn over the shirt from neck to waist and laces up the front with leather or velvet laces called points. Points are both decorative and functional. They tie the sleeve into the doublet and tie the upper sleeve to the lower sleeves. The shirt blouses at the shoulder and elbow and along the lower side of the arm. On top of the doublet, a hip-to thigh-length cape may be worn over one or both shoulders. A sleeved jerkin or long sleeveless vest may also be worn over the doublet and hose. A belt at the waist may hold a pouch or dagger.

Waist/Hip/Hose
Tights extend from waist to foot in a natural body line. Parti-colored patterns of stripes, chevrons, and other geometrics create a unique look. A flat piece of fabric called a codpiece ties to the hose to cover the space between the two separate stockings, which tie onto the belt with points.

Footwear
A comfortable flat-heeled lace-up shoe with a round toe is in keeping with the naturally rounded shapes of the rest of the silhouette. A midcalf, soft boot also follows the natural silhouette.

Late Renaissance

1520–1560

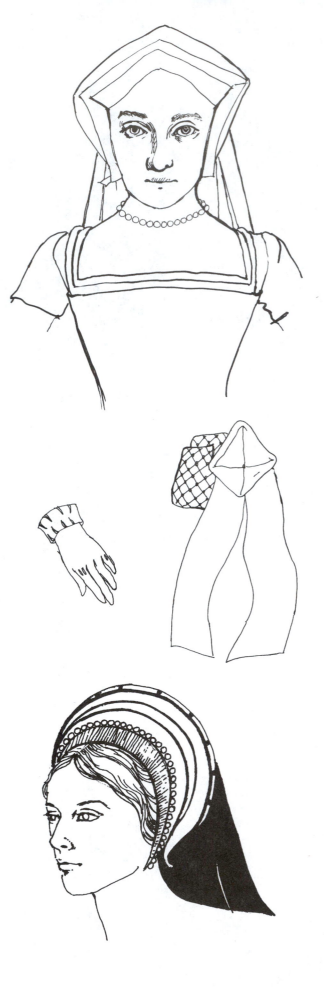

Headdress/Hair

The gable- or crescent-shaped headdress covers the hair except for the section above the forehead, which is parted in the center and pulled under the headdress. The headdress has a hood on the back, usually of black velvet, which covers the hair and falls to just above the waist in the back. It fastens under the chin with ties. Gold and jewels decorate the front of the headdress.

Neck/Shoulder/Arm

The gown has a wide, square neckline and a corseted, flat bodice. The sleeve is very narrow at the armhole and flares below the elbow with a wide cuff that turns back to the upper arm. A false inner sleeve with puffs and slashes on the lower arm ends at the wrist with a ruffle. Undergarments include a chemise, a corset that laces in back and has whalebone inset in the front, and petticoats.

Waist/Hip/Skirt

The waist is corseted in and has a V-shaped front. The skirts flare out, usually parting in the front to show an underskirt of contrasting fabric that usually matches the inner sleeve. Skirts are pleated at the waist and supported by a hip roll. The hem lengthens to a short train in the back. Often a chain around the waist continues down the front of the skirt and holds a pomander in a jeweled ball.

Footwear

Stockings and shoes barely show but follow the same fashion as the male with a square-toed slipper.

Late Renaissance

1520–1560

Headdress/Hair

Hairstyles are parted on the side, short, and trimmed either above or just below the ear. A carefully trimmed mustache and square-shaped beard are fashionable. The universal hat of the period is the flat-brimmed beret, which is worn slanted to one side of the head. It is decorated with a brooch and an ostrich plume.

Neck/Shoulder/Arm

The shirt is full, with gathered sleeves, smocked shoulder, and mandarin or ruffled collar. A stiff, square-necked doublet is worn over the shirt, and the doublet sleeves appear beneath the greatcoat sleeves. A sleeveless vest is worn over the doublet with a knee-length, cartridge-pleated skirt called bases. The width of the shoulder comes from the greatcoat (also called a robe or gown) which is frequently fur-lined. It has a large fur collar extending from the shoulder out over the sleeve and tapering down to the hem. A large puffed and padded sleeve ends just above the elbow. Men carry or wear gloves. A large chain necklace, or order, often goes across the collar of the greatcoat and the front of the doublet.

Waist/Hip/Skirt

The greatcoat extends from shoulder to knee and has a turned-back fur collar that continues in a lapel going down to the knee. Beneath the greatcoat, the pleated skirt ends above the knee. Tights cover the legs, usually with matching garters below the knee. A belt at the waist may have a jeweled dagger or purse attached. A padded codpiece is displayed between the front slit of the bases or tights.

Footwear

The square-toed, duck-billed shoe is distinctive to the Tudor period. It is a flat-heeled open shoe with a strap across the instep and a square, padded, and puffed shape at the toe. The leather is often slashed and bejeweled.

Elizabethan

1560–1590

Headdress/Hair

A high forehead is considered fashionable. Hair is brushed back and rolled over padding or a wire frame to create height. The back of the hair is upswept and arranged into a roll or bun to keep it out of the way of the high-standing ruff collar. Men and women wore similar hats. The hat has a narrow brim and a tall, soft, pleated-in crown. It is trimmed with braid, jewels, or feathers.

Neck/Shoulder/Arm

The neck ruff might be made of simple lawn or elaborate lace, starched and shaped into a figure-eight or ruffle effect. Ruffs vary from narrow to very wide and some ladies wear two or three at a time. The collar extends from under the chin tilting up to the back of the head. The tightly fitted bodice is worn over a flat, boned corset. The flat-chested, long-waisted bodice has a high or square neckline and fitted sleeves accompanied by hanging sleeves or bell-shaped oversleeves. Wide braid may trim bodice and skirt. Decorative puffs of fabric, often accentuated by jewels, adorn the sleeves and bodices. A wrist ruff matches the neck ruff. Shoulder crescents or wings accent the shoulder width where the sleeve attaches to the bodice. Rings, pins, necklaces abound and jeweled ornaments adorn bodices and skirts. Gloves and fans are important accessories.

Waist/Hip/Skirt

The corseted-in V-shaped waist has tabs or lapits extending over the waistband of the skirt. Petticoats and a hiproll, or a farthingale of wooden hoops, support the width of the skirt. The overskirt parts in the center to show an underskirt of different fabric.

Footwear

A low-heeled slipper ties in the front and has a wide shoe rose for decoration. Shoes and stockings are barely show because of the wide skirt.

Elizabethan

1560–1590

Headdress/Hair

Hairstyles are short, and tapered around the ear and hairline in the back. Narrow, shaped mustaches and neatly trimmed beards are popular. The universal hat of the period is a tall-puffed beret with a narrow, flat brim, which is worn tilted to one side of the head. The brim is often decorated with gold braid, plumes, and jewels.

Neck/Shoulder/Arm

The Elizabethan period is most easily identified by the starched ruff worn at the neck. It begins the period as a small ruffle on the neck of the shirt and becomes separate curved neckband made of lace sewn on in a figure-eight pattern. Widths vary from narrow to a very wide ruff that requires a wire support in the back. The doublet has a high neck and is very fitted through the shoulder and sleeve. Wings, or shoulder crescents, attach at the armseye where the sleeve joins the doublet. At the wrist a smaller ruff matches the one at the neck. Gloves are a fashionable necessity.

Waist/Hip/Breeches

The doublet comes to a slight V-waist and is often padded through the chest. A stiffened and curved peplum flares from the waist 3" to 7" over the round hose. Round hose, or breeches, extend from the waist to the upper thigh, supported by bombast or padding. Braid decorates edges of doublets and hose. Knee-length padded breeches, called canions, may be worn alone or under the round hose. Strips of contrasting fabric, called panes, are often worn over round hose. A short cape worn over one shoulder is hip-length. Knitted stockings, or lower hose, cover the lower leg. Swords or daggers are worn around the waist. Padded codpieces decorate the front of round hose.

Footwear

Men wear a natural shaped flat-heeled slipper tied in the front with decorative shoe-bows. Many shoes are slashed in a pattern similar to that on the doublets.

Late Elizabethan and Jacobean

1590–1620

Headdress/Hair

Hair is upswept in a heart-shaped or tightly curled style. Hats are similarly styled for women and men: a stiff-crowned, narrow-brimmed beaver hat with braid, plumes, and jewels for trim.

Neck/Shoulder/Arm

The high standing whisk collar flares out around the face. It has a wire support and is decorated with embroidery and jewels. The Elizabethan ruff continues to be a standard part of dress, and women sometimes wear both a whisk collar and a ruff. The sleeve and shoulder are tightly fitted. The sleeve ends with a wide flat cuff trimmed to match the collar. This combination of the whisk or ruff and the flat cuff is a characteristic of the Jacobean period. The sleeve may be puffed at the top and tapered to the wrist. Cuffs and collars are sometimes worn in double or triple sets. A second decorative hanging sleeve may be made from a flat piece of fabric extending from the shoulder almost to the floor. Shoulder crescents, or wings, attach to the shoulder where the sleeve joins the bodice, and they match the dress fabric. The bodice is long-waisted and flatly corseted in to a deep V-waist. Necklines are high or very low.

Waist/Hip/Skirt

The tightly corseted, deep V-shape waist contrasts with the wide-wheel farthingale skirt. Skirt supports include petticoats and a wheel farthingale, a boned, wheel-shaped support attached to the waist with tapes that holds the skirt out around the body. The gathered section of the skirt under the wheel shape is floor-length.

Footwear

Stockings and shoes rarely show because of the skirt width. A flat-heeled slipper ties in the front and has a shoe rose for decoration—a round flower-shaped arrangement of ribbons ranging from 3" to 6" and worn on the front of the shoe.

Late Elizabethan and Jacobean

1590–1620

Headdress/Hair

Hairstyles have natural curls and waves that are trimmed to just below the ears and at the nape of the neck. Small mustaches and trimmed, pointed beards are popular. Hats are fashionable and worn indoors and outdoors. The most popular style is the beaver hat with a tall, stiff crown, a narrow brim, a jeweled band, and ostrich plumes.

Neck/Shoulder/Arm

The whisk, a standing flat collar, is trimmed with lace and flares out around the back of the head. It is usually wired for support. The doublet is flat in front and tightly fitted through the shoulders and sleeves. The sleeve has a flat cuff trimmed with lace to match the collar. Shoulder crescents, or wings, attach at the shoulder where the sleeve joins the doublet. The fabrics used are brocades and complicated woven patterns. Men wear or carry gloves that have a flat cuff.

Waist/Hip/Breeches

The V-waist fits tightly, and shaped tabs overlap at the waist to cover the top of the Venetians, or canion breeches. The Venetians gather in at the waist and taper to a tight fit just above the knee. Venetians sometimes combined with round hose, or padded short hose that end at the top of the thigh. Embroidered clocks decorate the ankles of stockings. Ribbons may cross-garter at the knee.

Footwear

The T-strap slipper has a small French heel. Wide shoe roses decorate the front of the shoe and match the doublet and breeches. Tall, soft boots are worn for riding.

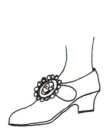

Cavalier

1620–1660

Headdress/Hair

The Cavalier woman wears fringed bangs across the forehead and ringlets or curls at the side of the face. Most of the hair is swept into a bun high at the back of the head. Hairstyles are soft and in natural colors. Indoors, women often wear small white cotton caps. For riding and dress occasions, a wide-brimmed hat with ribbon decoration or plumes is angled at one side of the head.

Neck/Shoulder/Arm

Matching cuffs and falling-band collar accent the neckline and wrist. The large collar extends from the neck to beyond the shoulder. It is made of simple linen, thick lace, or solid fabric trimmed with lace. The neckline is either high or low and rounded. The shoulder has a rounded shape created by the corset and bodice of this period. The sleeves are soft and puffed, starting just below the shoulder bone and reaching the wrist. Sleeves sometimes slash down the center front, revealing an inner sleeve of a different color. The short-waisted bodice corsets in to a flat front and small waist. The bodice usually has a peplum or overlapping tabs at the waist covering the waistband.

Waist/Hip/Skirt

The waistline corsets in to a small circumference. The full pleated skirt is supported by a roll bolster and several layers of petticoats. The front of the skirt reaches the floor, and the back of the skirt has a 4" to 6" brush train. The skirt, bodice, and sleeves are frequently trimmed with braid or ribbon.

Footwear

Stockings of wool, cotton, and silk barely show beneath the skirt. Brocade or leather slippers have a high instep and a 1" or 2" French or spool heel.

Cavalier

1620–1660

Headdress/Hair

Hair is straight or curly, shoulder-length, and layered, often with curled or fringed bangs. Hairstyles have a casual, natural look in both color and shape. Small mustaches and triangular beards are popular. The broad-brimmed beaver hat has a high crown and ribbon, braid, or ostrich plume trimming. The brim is soft and frequently turned up on one side. The beaver hat is either dark or pastel. The light tan and gray frequently match the bucket-top boots.

Neck/Shoulder/Arm

The falling-band collar is a distinguishing characteristic of the Cavalier costume. The collar falls from a curved band around the neck. It can be flat or gathered. The fullness is achieved by gathers or cartridge pleating. The collar may be lace, lace-trimmed, or a solid fabric and extends to the edge of the shoulder. Matching flat cuffs are of the same fabric and trimmings. Collars and cuffs are generally white or pastel.

The doublet is a short-waisted jacket ending in a V-shape at the front about 1" or 2" above the normal waistline. Large overlapping tabs or a 6"- to 10"-long peplum attach at the waist. Crescent-shaped pieces of fabric attach at the shoulder where the sleeve joins the doublet. The sleeve is puffed or semifull. Slashing on the sleeve and doublet frequently reveals contrasting fabrics.

Decorative braid often outlines the doublet, tabs, crescents, sleeves, collars, and cuffs. Ribbon bows at the waist and shoulder derive from the functional lacings that previously held garments together. Center front buttons are frequently left undone halfway down the doublet. A hip-length cape that ties over the doublet is usually worn off one shoulder at an asymmetrical angle. Every gentleman wears gloves.

Waist/Hip/Breeches

Pleated, full breeches gather in to a band above or below the knee. Braid or buttons trim the outside seam from waist to knee. Bows or ribbons decorate the bottom of the breeches above silk or cotton stockings. Swords and baldrics are part of every day dress.

Footwear

Bucket-top boots of soft leather and suede are worn for dress and for riding. The large cuff can be worn up on the thigh or turned down and filled with boot lace. Both boots and shoes are pastel or dark in color and have 2" heels and round toes. Shoes have cutout sides that create a T-strap effect. Large 3" to 5" ribbon or cloth shoe roses decorate the front of shoes.

Restoration

1660–1680

Headdress/Hair

Hairstyles are flat on top, parted in the center, and have very full ringlets and layered curls at the sides. Compared to men's long wigs, women's hair is soft and natural-looking. Ribbons are the major head-dress, and hats are rarely worn. A soft hood ties over the hair on occasion.

Neck/Shoulder/Arm

A heavily boned corset with a deep V-shape in the front emphasizes a small waist and a pushed-up bustline. The shoulder line is rounded. Rounded necklines are generally low and have ruffles or collars. Puffed sleeves with ruffles and ribbons end just below the elbow. Long-waisted flat bodices have a V-shaped stomacher covering the front lacings. Preferred jewels are pearl necklaces, earrings, and bracelets.

Waist/Hip/Skirt

Separate from the bodice, the skirt has deep pleats and is supported by a hip roll, or hip pad. This pad ties around the hip bone and supports the skirt in soft folds away from the body. The skirt may be one piece or may open in the front, with the sides held back to show the underskirt. The skirt hem touches the ground in front and tapers back to a 6" to 12" train.

Footwear

Stockings and shoes barely show. During this period, shoes begin to have a higher tongue in the front and are cut high on the instep. French heels are 2" to 2 $\frac{1}{2}$", and shoes are frequently made of a brocade that matches the gown.

Restoration

1660–1680

Headdress/Hair

The wig becomes fashionable for men during this period. It is natural in color and luxurious in length. Wigs and hair are parted in the center and waved and curled to fall over the shoulder and frequently halfway down the chest and back. A small mustache sometimes accompanies the wig. The wide-brimmed felt or beaver hat with a tall crown and a silk band has lavish decorations of ribbons and ostrich plumes. The steeple hat of the Puritans, a wide-brimmed hat with a taller and straighter crown, is also seen during this period.

Neck/Shoulder/Arm

Men wear the rabat, a flat, pleated-in collar, on a neckband at the center front of the neck. The cravat, a gathered-in fall of lace or fabric, is another popular neck accessory. It is usually worn falling over a wide bow tie at the chin. Men's shirts are full and flowing, particularly the sleeves. The sleeves gather in at the wrist and are trimmed with ribbons and lace. A shortwaisted, bolero-type jacket with sleeves ending above the elbow is worn over the shirt. The short sleeves of this rochet jacket often have turned-up cuffs. The shirt blouses out at the waist, and the flowing sleeves blouse out below the jacket sleeves. The shoulder line is natural. Leather or silk gloves are an important accessory.

Waist/Hip/Breeches

Knee-length petticoat breeches accompany the rochet jacket and blousy shirt. There are three major styles: a kilt-type skirt, a culotte-style divided full pants, and very full knee breeches called slops. All styles are decorated with ruffles or rows of ribbon loops, thus earning the name petticoat breeches. A wide ruffle falls from below the knee to mid-calf and covers a garter. Silk stockings are worn with the petticoat breeches. A knee-length circular cape with a flat collar may be worn over the jacket and breeches.

Footwear

A square-heeled shoe with a high tongue that extends past the ankle balances out this silhouette. The toe is square, and the front of the shoe sports a 6" to 8" wide, stiffened bow that matches the ribbons trimming the shirt and breeches.

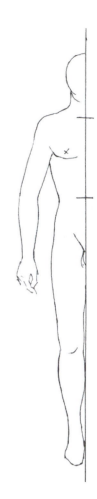

Baroque

1680–1715

Headdress/ Hair

The Fontanges headdress distinguishes the women's Baroque costume. A series of tiered and wired ruffles or ribbons stand upright 6" or 8" or may angle forward on the head. They attach to a lace or fabric cap worn on the back of the head. Streamers or ribbons from the back of the cap fall to the middle of the back. The hair is worn high and formal, with curls dressed over a wire frame and symmetrical curls or each side of the forehead. The back section of hair is in a bun, with long finger curls falling on each side of the shoulder.

Neck/Shoulder/Arm

Women are tightly corseted. The corset uplifts the bustline and narrows the waist to a deep V-shape. The neckline of the bodice is square. A square short sleeve with a wide cuff ends above the elbow. A ruffled or puffed inner sleeve of contrasting fabric extends to below the elbow. Matching bracelets and elbow-length gloves decorate the lower arm. The bodice opens center front. This opening is covered by a stomacher, a separate V-shaped piece with contrasting fabric or ribbon trimmings. Pearl earrings and necklaces, and possibly beauty spots, complete the silhouette. Women carry fans in most social situations.

Waist/Hip/Skirt

The new look created during this period is to pull the overskirt to the side or center back, creating a bustle effect and a 2' to 3' train at the back of the skirt. The underskirt, usually of a different color and fabric, may be decorated with ruffles or braid and lace trimmings.

Footwear

Stockings are silk or cotton. Shoes have a 2" to 3" French or spool heel and a high tongue in the front. Shoes are frequently made from brocade or embroidered leather.

Baroque

1680–1715

Headdress/Hair

A full and elaborate wig dominates the male silhouette. It has high 3" to 4" curls on the forehead and is parted in the center. The wig frequently ends 2" or 3" below the shoulder or just above the waist in the back. A felt or beaver hat has a wide brim, but the crown is low, only 3" to 4". Braid, ribbon, and ostrich plumes lavishly decorate this important accessory.

Neck/Shoulder/Arm

The neckstock is a cravat or Steinkirk. The cravat, a gathered fall of lace 8" to 10" long, combines with a large stiffened bow tie under the chin. This is appropriately called the cat's whiskers bow tie. The Steinkirk is a long neckcloth looped at the neck and twisted to tuck in midway down the front of the coat.

The coat is knee-length, flared below the waist, and has side and back vents. The coat has a round cardigan-type neckline. The front of the coat has large buttons and buttonholes from neck to hem. Sleeves fit from shoulder to elbow and have large cuffs extending from midarm to above the wrist. These cuffs have 2" to 3" decorative buttons and buttonholes or the upper edge of the cuff that match those on the front of the coat.

A shirt is worn beneath the coat, but only a ruffle of lace or fabric shows at the wrist. A sleeveless waistcoat, or vest, is knee-length, ending 1" or 2" shorter than the coat. The vest is made of contrasting fabric and has decorative buttons from neck to hem. Handkerchiefs, gloves, snuffboxes, swords, walking sticks, and large muffs are accessories that fashionable gentlemen use to display the elaborate manners and protocol of the period.

Waist/Hip/Breeches

Knee breeches pleat at the waist and have gathered fullness just above or below the knee. Stockings roll over the knee, and elaborate garters are usually worn below the knee. Large, wide decorative pockets appear on the skirt of the coat above the front hem. Wide flaps with decorative buttons and buttonholes go over the pocket.

Footwear

Shoes have a square heel and toe. A large tongue on the front of the shoe reaches above the ankle and has a buckle or wide bow on the front.

Rococo

1715–1774

Headdress/Hair

The Rococo period has lighter colors and trimmings than the very ornate Baroque/Louis XIV period. The first noticeable difference is the white color of both men's and women's hair and wigs. In the early Rococo period women's hair is powdered and worn close to the head in small curls. In the later Rococo period powdered hairstyles take on great height, and white or light-gray wigs become fashionable. Women wear ribbons and real or artificial flowers in their hair. Hats include the mob cap, a small white cap with ruffled edges and a gathered crown. Women wear the cap by itself or under a low-crowned, flat-brimmed straw hat that ties under the chin. The face is powdered white, and rouge and lipstick are in vogue.

Neck/Shoulder/Arm

The neckline is soft and usually adorned with a small ruff of lace or ribbon. The narrow and boned bodice corsets in with a flat front and narrow waist. The bustline pushes up to form a décolletage. The gown opens in the front. A decorated stomacher goes either under or over the front opening and displays graduated rows of silk bows. Armholes are small, and sleeves are fitted. Sleeves extend to just above the elbow where two or three rows of wide ruffles or lace fall gracefully over the lower arm. A matching pair of ribbons or bracelets adorns the wrists. The neckline shape is a square or sweetheart, and the waistline shape is a slight V. Many gowns have Watteau pleats, deep folds of fabric from the neckline to the hem in the back.

Waist/Hip/Skirt

The skirt dominates the silhouette of this period. It is flat in front and back and supported by a pannier, a basket or boned structure that fits on the sides of the body. The pannier supports the skirt a few inches from the side of the body. An overskirt flares out over the pannier and opens in front to reveal an elaborately embroidered or decorated underskirt. The underskirt usually clears the ground in front, and the overskirt sweeps into a train in back.

Footwear

A silk brocade shoe with pointed toe and curved high heel is as elaborate as the dress. Heels could be up to 3" high.

Rococo

1715–1774

Headdress/Hair

Men wear or carry the tricorne, or three-cornered hat, throughout this period. It is usually black and trimmed with braid or ribbon. Hair is powdered to a light gray or white. Hair and wigs are worn full and to the shoulder at the beginning of the period. After 1730 hair is pulled to the back of the head into a black silk bag or a ponytail style. Large sausage-style curls are arranged above the ear in two or three rows. They are frequently rolled over pads to create more fullness.

Neck/Shoulder/Arm

Men's shirts vary in fabric from cotton muslin to silk crepe. They have a round or band-shaped neckline, a drop shoulder, and full sleeves finished with ruffles or lace at the wrist. The jabot, worn at the neck of the shirt, is a neckband with three or four rows of ruffles falling down the chest. The solitaire is a black silk bow tie. It extends from the bag covering the hair at the back of the head and ties in a bow at the front.

The waistcoat fits close to the body and reaches midthigh. It has buttons from neck to hem and is made from contrasting brocade or other fabric. The coat has a cardigan neckline and is open in the front. The coat skirts are cut back at an angle to reveal the waistcoat and breeches. Shoulders are narrow, and armseyes are small. The sleeve is narrow and ends in a large cuff 4" to 6" above the wrist. The shirt sleeve blouses over the hand and finishes with ruffles at the wrist. The cuff is trimmed with braid, buttons, and buttonholes to match the front of the coat. The snuffbox, gloves, handkerchief, and walking stick are necessary accessories.

Waist/Hip/Breeches

Breeches are full at the waist and usually buckled at the center back to allow flexibility for waist size. The legs of the breeches fit snugly on the knee and lower thigh. They button on the outside, just below the knee. White cotton or silk stockings extend from under the breeches and cover the leg. The coat skirt has full pleats at the side, matching the look of the panniers in the women's skirts. By the 1770s, the skirt of the coat narrows, creating a more slender look.

Footwear

Men wear a black, flat-heeled pump with a front buckle. The riding boot is knee-length or higher with a flat heel and round toe.

Neoclassic

1775–1789

Headdress/Hair

Many styles of wigs and powdered hair distinguish the silhouette. The sides are wide and full, and the top of the hair frequently achieves great height. Hair is curled over most of the head, and finger curls usually adorn each side of the neck. After 1780 wigs start to go out of style and hair has less height and more fullness at the sides. English styles are more modest than French styles. Hairstyles are topped with wide-brimmed hats, lavishly trimmed with feathers and ribbons. They tilt to one side of the head to make a lovely frame for the coiffure and face. The mob cap, a gathered and ruffled soft cap, is made in sheer silk fabrics as well as cottons and worn during this period sometimes even on top of a high wig.

Neck/Shoulder/Arm

Many changes of style take place during this period because of Marie Antoinette's great influence upon fashion. Gowns are worn over a chemise, corset, petticoats, and hip roll. Four popular gowns are the polonaise, the court gown, the Gainsborough look, and the redingote. The polonaise gown has a long-waisted, boned bodice, which hooks up the front. The sleeve fits tightly in the armhole and is elbow- or wrist-length. A sheer fichu, a type of scarf that ties loosely around the neck and shoulder, decorates the low curved neckline. A tailored, double-breasted jacket identifies the redingote gown. It has wide lapels and a sleeve fitted to the wrist. Buttons on the sleeve match those on the jacket.

The court gown, named for the French court, has a low neckline and fitted bodice with sleeves to the elbow finished by three rows of ruffled lace or fabric. The Gainsborough gown has a fitted bodice, frill-length fitted sleeve and a higher round neckline. A fichu may accompany this style also.

Waist/Hip/Skirt

The polonaise gown emphasizes the corseted-in waist with a gathered-in underskirt and the polonaise overskirt, which is pulled up in swags with cords on the underside of the skirt. It may also be supported by panniers, hoops, or pads on the side of the body. This skirt usually is midcalf or ankle-length, a "working class" look. The redingote gown is a tailored coat dress that opens up in front. The floor-length skirt often parts to show an underskirt of another color. The court gown has a V-waist and a skirt supported by panniers that may go up to 3'

in width on each side of the body. It is flat on the front and back, usually comprising an underskirt and swagged overskirt. The skirt on the Gainsborough gown is gathered and soft supported only by petticoats. The waist is a soft V-shape and the skirt is floor-length.

Footwear

Light-colored stockings show under the shorter skirts of the polonaise gown. The shoe is a 2" to 3" French-heeled pump in brocaded silks or other fabrics matching the gown. A buckle frequently decorates the high instep of the shoe.

Neoclassic

1775–1789

Headdress/Hair

In this extravagant Louis XVI period both men and women wear wigs. The men's wig is powdered white or gray, has sausage rolls on the side of the head, and pulls back into several styles of ponytails or pigtails. Favorite headwear includes the tricorne hat, a three-cornered black felt hat smaller in width than those popular in the Rococo period, and a flat-topped hat with a rolled brim. By the late 1780s the steeple-crowned hat, named for its tall crown, appears. After 1785 the bicorne hat appears.

Neck/Shoulder/Arm

The ruffled cravat or the wrapped neckstock appears at the top of the vest or waistcoat. The vest is long, reaching about 6" or 7" below the waist. The shirt only appears at the wrist with ruffles of lace or other fabric. The coat shoulders fit with a natural line, and the collar lies flat around the neck. Sleeves are straight and decorated at the wrist with buttons and braid. This form of the coat fits across the upper chest and then curves to the back, revealing the upper leg. Large flat buttons decorate the front of the coat. Fabrics range from silk brocades for the court to woolen twills for the middle classes.

Waist/Hip/Breeches

Breeches fit tightly on the hip and thigh, ending at the knee with a buckle or button. Breeches are made of jersey, buckskin, and other fabrics that are cut on the bias to create this smooth fit.

Footwear

Country or military dress requires well-fitted riding boots. The flat-heeled dress pump has a square buckle on the front. Stockings are usually white.

Directoire

1790–1799

Headdress/Hair

Although powdered wigs abound in the previous period, natural hair colors and more relaxed styles are the standard for this period. Hairstyles vary from the classic chignon, with curls at the side of the head, to a fringed and layered short cut. In between are styles with soft ringlets at the front and sides of the head and lengths of hair pulled back in various styles.

Many forms of headdress are fashionable in this turbulent period in the early part of the French revolution. Turbans and the coal-scuttle and poke bonnets are especially popular. The steeple-crown hat and large- and small-brimmed straw hats have ribbons, ostrich plumes, feathers, wheat stalks, and flowers for trimming.

Neck/Shoulder/Arm

The fichu, a large scarf wrapped around the neck, crosses the bustline and fastens into the belt or ties in the back. Undergarments include soft chemises, corsets, and petticoats gathered with fullness at the back. The hip roll worn early in the decade disappears by its end. The shoulder is narrow, as are the elbow- or wrist-length sleeves. The waistline is natural in 1790, but the short-waisted look is in style by 1795. Shawls, stoles, reticule or purse, and gloves are common accessories. Fashionable bracelets, necklaces, and rings accompany the dress.

Waist/Hip/Skirt

The open robe, or gown, of cotton or silk may part in front to show an underskirt. The gown, which touches the top of the shoe, has most of its fullness gathered at the back of the skirt. A sash or wide ribbon frequently decorates the waist and may tie in a bow in the back.

Footwear

Silk or cotton stockings combine with a flat-heeled, pointed-toe leather slipper. Stockings sometimes have embroidery at the ankle called clocks. Shoes and sandals frequently lace above the ankle.

Directoire

1790–1799

Headdress/Hair

Wigs are no longer fashionable. The back of the hair is cut short, and the sides are often combed forward creating a wind-blown look. The top of the hair is elevated by teasing. Fringed bangs are worn across the forehead in an uneven effect. Hats are usually black beaver or felt. Two major hat shapes dominate. The first is the steeple crown, a hat with a small buckle or ribbon trim, a 2" brim, and a 6" to 10" crown. The second is the bicorne, a hat with a wide brim that is turned up on both sides to form two corners. Braid or ribbon may decorate the edges.

Neck/Shoulder/Arm

A wide, wrapped neckstock that ties in front covers the neck up to and sometimes over the chin. A neckband shirt is worn under a waist-length vest. The double- or single-breasted vest is cut high, just below the collarbone. It often has a collar and lapels. Made of bright colors, the vest contrasts with the coat. A high-standing collar on the coat extends just below the ear. The coat has wide lapels, is single- or double-breasted, and is knee-length. The frock coat extends straight across in the front above the knee. The cutaway is cut square across the chest 3" or 4" above the waist; it then slants down the side of the body. Shoulders are naturally fitted, and a straight sleeve frequently ends in a turned-back half-cuff.

Waist/Hip/Breeches

The breeches, or culottes, end below the knee and have button fastenings in front of the waist and at the knee. They are full at the hip and narrow at the knee. Patterned, striped, or plain white knit stockings cover the leg.

Footwear

Boots have a low, square heel and are of various heights. The soft leather low-cut shoe has a semi-pointed toe and ribbon trim.

Empire

1800–1815

Headdress/Hair

The new classical but casual hairstyles include ringlets and chignons, as well as curls around the face and fringed bangs. Jockey bonnets, poke bonnets, wide-brimmed straw hats, and wrapped turbans constitute favorite hat styles. Silk ribbons and artificial roses and flowers adorn evening hairstyles.

Neck/Shoulder/Arm

The Empire gown, or chemise, usually has a round neckline. In the early part of the period, the neckline is created with a drawstring. Later, the gown has a short bodice of shaped pieces with a round or V-shaped neckline and a collar. The short puffed sleeve is a new look for both day and evening and frequently is accompanied by elbow-length gloves. For day, the puffed sleeve often has a wrist-length semifitted sleeve under it, or a puffed sleeve tapering to the wrist.

Waist/Hip/Skirt

The high-waisted gown is the mark of the Empire silhouette. The skirt is flat in front and gathered in the back. The back of the skirt is often cartridge-pleated and supported by crinoline ruffles to help the fullness fall gracefully away from the back of the body. The hemline brushes the top of the shoe or comes to just above the ankle and is moderately full.

Footwear

Stockings are white or flesh-colored. Shoes called escarpins resemble today's ballet slipper. Shoes are narrow with a pointed or square toe and a thin sole, and they frequently are cross-laced on the leg above the ankle like a Grecian sandal.

Empire

1800–1815

Headdress/Hair

The tall beaver top hat comes into fashion and remains a major part of men's headwear throughout the nineteenth century. Another hat, the bicorne made famous by Napoleon, is a two-cornered hat in a variety of sizes and trimmings. Hairstyles are wind-blown and nonaristocratic looking. They are inspired by the images of Roman emperors that Napoleon imitated during his rule. Hair is brushed or combed forward in fringed bangs around the face. It is often teased and lacquered on the top of the head to create height.

Neck/Shoulder/Arm

The high, two-point collar turns up around the chin, and a wrapped cravat ties in front. The shirt and collared waistcoat show in the front. The coat is single- or double-breasted, with a collar and lapels that roll up around the back of the neck. The shoulder is moderately padded, and the sleeve is fitted to the wrist. The coat, a form of the cutaway, is most commonly tapered from the front waist to the side and cut back into square tails. It ends above the knee in the back of the figure.

Waist/Hip/Trousers

The cutaway coat has a slim hip and is worn over long, tight-fitting pantaloons, or trousers. Popularized by Beau Brummell, the style of ankle-length trousers continues for two hundred years in various shapes. The bottom of the trousers usually falls over the top of the shoe and fastens under the shoe or boot with a strap. Some trousers stop at the ankle. Tightly fitted knee breeches appear briefly as court dress.

Footwear

Along with leather boots for military and outdoor wear, the distinctive footwear is the flat, black slipper, or escarpin. It is a low-cut slip-on pump with a pointed or wedge-shaped toe and is often trimmed with a flat grosgrain bow.

Romantic

1815–1848

Headdress/Hair

The soft, round look of the Romantic period features hair parted in the center with curls and fullness to the side of the head and curls on the forehead. At the midpoint of the Romantic period hairstyles include curls and loops of hair 6" to 8" high on the top of the head. Wigs are fashionable and frequently decorated with flowers, ribbons, and frothy trimmings. Bonnets prevail as the favorite headwear; sun and poke bonnets are made from cloth and straw. These bonnets have higher crowns and wide brims, perhaps to hold more decoration and to visually balance the extra width of women's skirts. Turbans become popular, and elaborate trimmings and height are built into evening hairstyles.

Neck/Shoulder/Arm

In the Romantic silhouette, the long swanlike neck is the ideal. This illusion is helped by dropping the sleeve past the shoulder point onto the top of the arm. This dropped shoulder combines with a round, oval or swan-shaped neckline. A puffed sleeve starts about 2" past the shoulder. The sleeve is short or above the elbow for evening and puffed at the shoulder and tapered to the wrist for daytime. The sleeve becomes progressively fuller from the 1820s to the 1830s, reaching its widest point in 1835 and then becoming more modest in the 1840s. The width of the puffed sleeve is supported by an inner sleeve and crinoline stiffening to a width of 12" to 18".

Waist/Hip/Skirt

The return of the tightly corseted waist, huge sleeves, and wide skirt marks the hourglass silhouette of the Romantic period. Belts emphasize a tiny waist. Bodices fit tightly over corsets and fasten down the back with lacings or hooks and eyes. The bell-shaped skirt is supported at the sides and back by a crescent-shaped roll bolster and several petticoats. The waist of the skirt is slightly above the normal waistline, and the skirt reaches just above or below the ankle. In the 1840s the skirt becomes floor-length.

Footwear

White stockings and a flat ballet-type slipper lace over the instep and up the ankle to complete the Romantic look. This slipper, called an escarpin, has a wedge-shaped or tapered toe.

Romantic

1815–1848

Headdress/Hair

Loose curls at the sides and back of the head reach the top of the coat collar. Long sideburns indicate the beginning of the Romantic style. Hairstyles get gradually longer during the 1820s and into the 1830s and include center and side parts, with the top of the hair often waved. A tall top hat with a curled brim is the predominant hat for day and evening. The top hat is made of beaver, straw, and silk in gray, black, or brown.

Neck/Shoulder/Arm

The collar appears above the wrapped neckstock and waistcoat. The shirt shows at the neck and wrist. Both the frock and tailcoats have high-standing collars of various types. The male silhouette mimics the female hourglass shape during the Romantic period. The coat takes on a puffed leg-of-mutton sleeve; it is full at the shoulder and tapers to fit the lower arm.

Waist/Hip/Trousers

The full-skirted frock coat can be single- or double-breasted and shows off a cinched-in waist which is achieved by a corset or a waist cincher. The waistcoat often has a padded chest. The trousers frequently include pleats at the hip and even small hip pads to achieve the hourglass shape. Trousers are made in two major styles: a long tubular style with a strap under the instep, and bell-bottoms fitted on the thigh and flared below the knee. Trousers do not have cuffs or creases.

Footwear

Most men wear a low-cut pump or slipper with a flat heel and rounded or wedge-shaped toe. White stockings are worn with the leather pump or slipper. Boots continue to be used for riding and military wear.

Crinoline

1840–1868

Headdress/Hair

Center-parted hair is pulled flat into a chignon at the back of the head. Long ringlets or finger curls fall from the ear to the shoulder in another favorite hairstyle. This style is also parted in the center and flat at the top of the head. A bonnet frequently adorns the head and balances the silhouette with the full skirt below. The leghorn straw picture hat also frames the face in an attractive way. Flowers and ribbons adorn formal evening hairstyles.

Neck/Shoulder/Arm

The long neck of the Romantic period is still the ideal. Soft shoulders are rounded, as are most necklines. Necklines are high for daytime and low, even off the shoulder, for evening. Evening styles include a small cap or puffed sleeve that leaves the arm bare, but the hands are always gloved. Day sleeves extend to the wrist and are fitted or puffed. They include the distinctive pagoda or funnel-shaped sleeve, which fits closely on the upper arm and flares below the elbow in a wide curve.

Waist/Hip/Skirt

The waistline corsets in to create the ideal hourglass silhouette. The dress waistline appears at the naturally smallest area of the waist, which is midway between the lower rib and the hip bone, and comes to a V shape in front.. The major focus of the Crinoline silhouette is the bell-shaped or half-circle skirt created by starched crinoline petticoats. The skirt is often reinforced by horsehair or by petticoats with steel hoops that support the skirt easily in widths of 3' to 6'. Over this support goes a very full skirt, often created with tiers of ruffles or with gathers of cartridge pleating. The skirt falls to the floor and for evening includes a small 12" to 18" train in back.

Footwear

The high-top shoe with a rounded toe, and a 1 $\frac{1}{2}$" to 2" heel appears during this period. It laces or buttons in the front or on the side and rises about 6" above the ankle. The same heel appears on the evening pump. Day shoes tend to be black or brown leather, but evening pumps may appear in pastel colors matching the dress.

Crinoline

1840–1868

Headdress/Hair

Hair is not as curly or wavy as in the Romantic period, but it continues to reach the top of the coat collar. Sideburns or side whiskers are sometimes very full. Hair is parted in the center or on the side and is smooth across the forehead. The top hat changes height and shape but continues to be the most popular headwear. The very tall stovepipe hat appears in the 1860s for day and evening wear. For informal wear, the bowler, a hat with a rounded crown, comes into style.

Neck/Shoulder/Arm

The coat shoulders are broader and squarer than the drop shoulder of the Romantic period and the shirt collar is generally lower. Coats button high, just under the collarbone, as does the waistcoat. A cravat ties in a narrow bow as one form of neckwear. The sleeve loses the Romantic puff and is either straight or fitted to the wrist. Collars and lapels are flat and moderately wide.

Waist/Hip/Trousers

Coats have lost the cinched-in waist full skirt and take on a straight line. The frock coat is usually double-breasted and extends to the knee; the waistline is low. Trousers are tubular and long, reaching almost to the floor at the back and slanting up to the front of the shoe. The tailcoat is now required for formal evening wear and continues for formal daywear.

Footwear

The low pump continues for evening. For daywear, a high lace-up or button-up shoe or the Wellington, a low-cut slip-on boot with elastic insets at the sides, is favored.

Bustle

1868–1890

Headdress/Hair

The hairstyles echo the bustle skirts they accompany. Hair is flat on the sides with height at the back of the head in chignons, ringlets and clusters of curls often created with false hair pieces added to the coiffure. Ringlets on the forehead and fringe bangs are popular. Small elaborately decorated hats were tipped forward on the diagonal tilting toward the face. In the 1880s hats slope more to the back of the head and are secured by hat pins or by ribbons under the chin. Feathers, stuffed birds, ribbons, and elaborate trimmings decorate these hats.

Neck/ Shoulder/Arm

A deep V neckline, both front and back, adorns evening dresses. The modest daytime jackets and bodices used the smaller V neckline or the high-standing band collar. Daytime sleeves are three-quarter or full-length with ruffles at the wrist and 3" to 4" of braid or trimmings on the sleeve's edge. The shoulder is narrow and a fitted two-piece sleeve is used. Evening dresses are sleeveless or with a small cap sleeve accompanied by elbow-length gloves.

Waist/Hip/Skirt

Corsets encase the waist, and the bodice or jacket is close-fitting and smoothly form-revealing. The bustle extension and train at the back of the skirt are the focus of the whole silhouette. The skirt is flat in the front and on the sides; bustle pads, wire cages, or boned skirts add extensions to the lower back of the body during the 1870s and from 1883 to 1889. For a short period around 1880, a tubular shape is fashionable. The bustle skirt is an elaborate engineering feat of drapery, ruffles, swags, flounces, and pleating decorated with ribbons, flowers, fringe, and lace. In the 1870s a 1' to 2' train completes the back of the bustle skirt.

Footwear

The high-top shoe of the Crinoline period continues in the Bustle period, with a medium heel for daywear. A low-cut, medium-heel pump is used for evening. Stockings are black or dark colors with light colors for evening.

Bustle

1868–1890

Headdress/Hair

Beards and mustaches continue to be fashionable but are more closely trimmed than in the Romantic and Crinoline periods. However, sideburns continue along the jawline. The hair, trimmed neatly around the ear, is shaved and tapered at the back of the head. Hair is longer on the top of the head. The top hat is worn with morning, frock, or tail coats. Hat choices, including the derby, bowler, and straw boater, abound to complete business attire.

Neck/Shoulder/Arm

The high-standing collar, gray and white striped ascot tie, and waistcoat complete morning or frock coats. They elegantly emphasize the neck. The square padding and shaping of the shoulder line creates an elegant coat. The sleeve is straighter and less fitted than in the Crinoline period. The four-button business suit has a flat notched collar and lapels. A matching waistcoat, standing collar, and cravat tie complete the silhouette. The Norfolk or belted jacket is proper dress for hunting or country outings.

Waist/Hip/Trousers

A straight-line frock coat replaces the corseted-in waistline of the Romantic period. The frock coat reaches to the knee, and the sack, or business suit, reaches the hip. Trousers are straight and tubular, falling to the top of the shoe in front and tapering back in a slant to the heel of the shoe. Knee breeches are worn as part of hunting attire with knee socks or gaiters covering the lower leg.

Footwear

The high-top lace-up or button-up shoe continues, as does the Wellington, a low slip-on boot with elastic insets on the side. Spats, a covering that goes over men's shoes, are usually light gray or tan. They button up the sides, strap under the foot, and cover the ankle. The low-cut evening pump continues for formal evening wear.

1890s

1890–1900

Headdress/Hair

The hair is slightly full above the ears and upswept into a soft, loose chignon often called the Gibson girl look, after the famous drawings by Charles Dana Gibson. This hairstyle also includes soft curls around the face. Hats include the flat straw boater and the wide-brimmed picture hat in straw, velvet, or felt with feather and flower trimmings.

Neck/Shoulder/Arm

A long neck is desirable, and daytime clothing carries a high collar with 1 1/2" to 2" boning or flexible wires to create this look. Evening necklines are curved low to a round or V shape. The shoulder look is square, with large, puffed, leg-of-mutton sleeves. Ruffles and trimmings at the shoulder create a high, square look. The sleeve flares beyond the shoulder, extends out over the upper arm, and narrows on the lower arm. Sleeves are wrist-length for day, and above the elbow or short, full, and puffed for evening. The latter often require three yards of fabric each and are stiffened or held out by crinolines and inner linings.

Waist/Hip/Skirt

The waist corsets in to a small circumference with a V shape in front. The rib cage is flat, and the bustline is pushed high. The hip area is flat and smooth on the side and the front. The skirt is gored instead of gathered so that it fits smoothly around the hips. Deep pleats create fullness at the center back of the skirt. The skirt flares to 3' to 4' in diameter at the hem, which is 1" to 2" off the floor. The back of the skirt frequently has a slight train of 3" to 6". The skirt flares from waist to hem to match the width of the sleeves at the bustline.

Footwear

The appearance of a small foot is desirable and thus the shoe is narrow, with a semipointed toe and a 1 1/2" to 2" medium heel. Most daytime shoes are high-top and either button or lace. Silk-covered evening shoes have a medium heel.

1890s

1890–1900

Headdress/Hair

At the end of the century, men's hair becomes short at the sides and the back, is parted in the center or on the side, and is brushed back. Small mustaches remain, but the clean-shaven look is predominant. Hats have variety and style. Formal wear requires the top hat, and the bowler or derby are accessories for informal wear. The Homburg, a predecessor to the twentieth-century fedora, appears. The light-colored straw boater and the Panama hat are popular for summer. Soft, billed caps appear in many styles for golf, tennis, and other sporting occasions.

Neck/Shoulder/Arm

Wing-tip, high-standing, and turnover collars are attached to neckband shirts. Soft, turn-down collars now become equally acceptable. Shirts are white for formal wear, but the striped shirt is popular for sport and business wear. The ascot and bow tie continue in fashion, and the four-in-hand takes equal precedence. The waistcoat comes in a variety of colors and patterns and in both single- and double-breasted styles. The square shoulder and slender sleeve complete frock, morning, and tail coats and also the new sportswear, including the Norfolk jacket, sack suit, and blazer. Overcoats include the velvet-collared Chesterfield.

Waist/Hip/Trousers

Tubular trousers become slender and some have creases. Knickers, or knee breeches, accompany the Norfolk or blazer jacket for hunting, golfing, and other sports. Thick stockings and frequently gaiters or spats complete the leg. Suspenders, or braces, appear with striped shirts.

Footwear

White or tan shoes and the lower-cut oxford appear for warm weather and sports. Business and work shoes are still high-top styles. Riding boots are knee-high. The evening tail coat requires the low-cut pump, often of patent leather. Spats cover the shoe for all daytime formal wear. They go over the oxford or lace-up shoe.

Edwardian

1900–1909

Headdress/Hair

Although many changes occur during this decade, the hair stays upswept in a pompadour with fullness at the sides and some height at the top called the Gibson girl style. The wide-brimmed picture hat with plumes and feathers completes the formal day silhouette. The flat-brimmed straw boater is a favorite hat for business and bicycling. As in the late nineteenth century, hats are considered proper attire anytime a woman is outside of the house.

Neck/Shoulder/Arm

A high-standing collar defines the neckline during most of this decade. Evening gowns have a lower neckline, and ladies often wear wide choker pearls to give the same effect. The bustline drops lower, and the neck and shoulders take on a long, elegant look. In general, the sleeve is narrower; it has a small puff at the shoulder during the first half of the decade. In 1903 and 1904 sleeves are slender at the shoulder and blouse below the elbow. Accessories include gloves, which are considered proper attire for day and evening.

Waist/Hip/Skirt

The waistline rises at the center back and dips just below the natural waistline in front to give it a diagonal shape. The body corsets in to an S curve with the dropped bustline in front and a narrow waist. The skirt is flat in front with fullness shirred in at the center back. Continuing flat throughout the hips, the skirt flares below the knee with pleats, ruffles, or gores and generally has a slight train at the back.

Footwear

Daytime wear is a high-top shoe that laces or buttons to the lower calf and has a pointed toe. The evening shoe is a low-heeled pump that often has a bow on the front. A low-cut, lace-up walking shoe appears toward the end of the decade.

Edwardian

1900–1909

Headdress/Hair

Hair is generally parted on the side and short on the sides and at the back. Mustaches are popular early in the period. Men wear the top hat for formal day wear as well as in the evening. Business wear includes the derby and the fedora. Soft, billed caps are worn with knickers for sporting occasions.

Neck/Shoulder/Arm

A high starched collar in several styles accents the neckline. The wing-tip collar accompanies the black and white striped ascot tie for formal wear. The round turnover collar is worn with the Windsor or bow tie for business and less formal occasions. The waistcoat is worn for business dress in the early part of the decade. The shoulder of frock and morning coats is lightly padded and shaped. Collars and lapels are medium width and jackets have 3 or 4 buttons. Sleeves are slightly curved and fall straight from shoulder to wrist. The cuff of the shirt shows about 1" at the wrist.

Waist/Hip/Trousers

Frock coats fall to just above the knee. Sack suit and Norfolk jackets reach the top of the thigh. Trousers are flat at the waist and usually held up by suspenders. During this period trousers become creased center front and back for the first time and also begin to have cuffs. The waistcoat, or vest, covers the waistline under the coat and over the shirt. Day vests are cut high and come just below the necktie. Evening vests are cut lower and show more of the shirt. Knickers, trousers that end at the knee with gathers and a band, are worn with knee socks. Gaiters or spats accompany the knee socks and cover the shoe for country or sports wear.

Footwear

High-top shoes that lace or button above the ankle are the most common footwear. Spats, a cloth or felt cover that buttons on the outside of the shoe, covers the top of the shoe and the ankle. They are usually worn with formal day wear. Evening dress is a low pump.

Teens

1910–1919

Headdress/Hair

Hair is upswept in a French roll or twist. Some styles are pulled up into a topknot or back into a bun. Hair is frequently waved smoothly at the side of the head. Hats vary in size from smaller hats to extremely wide-brimmed hats between 1912 and 1915. Styles popular from 1916 to 1918 include tailored, flat-brimmed sailor hats, turbans, and high toques. During this entire period millinery is trimmed with exotic feathers and plumes, such as aigrettes, paradise feathers, and whole bird wings. These trimmings are also fashionable hairdressing for evening wear.

Neck/Shoulder/Arm

A wide variety of styles is available in women's necklines. Tailored suits with lapels and collars and a variety of blouses are seen throughout the decade. These include walking suits, business suits, sports ensembles, and country suits. The high collars are still worn in 1911 but disappear mid-decade. Softer necklines are seen on kimono-style dresses with dolman sleeves, which are cut with the dress in one piece and give a soft, rounded shoulder. Shirtwaist blouses are worn with skirts with Windsor or bow ties at the neckline. Sleeves may be long, as on suits, but are elbow-length and even shorter on dresses. Evening gowns are short-sleeved or sleeveless.

Waist/Hip/Skirt

Waistlines vary along with other fashion elements during this period. Some waistlines are slightly raised in 1910 and 1911 but tend to be at a normal position by 1914 and 1915. Skirts are ankle-length in 1910 but by 1916 rise to midcalf, where they stay until the end of the decade. Some suits have hip-length jackets. Dresses and suits are often belted. Skirts are straight or just slightly flared on both suits and dresses. A long corset or girdle flattens the hips. Stockings are seamed cotton or silk and begin to be visible as the hemline rises. The hobble skirt and lampshade skirt are some of the unusual skirts from this period.

Footwear

The high-top shoe is worn through most of the decade but begins to be replaced by the lower cut pump and the 2" spool-heel, lace-up oxford for day and business wear. Spats give the look of a high-top shoe when they are worn over a pump. They slip over the shoe and button up the outside of the leg, reaching above the ankle. Low pumps are worn for evening.

Teens

1910–1919

Headdress/Hair

Side-parted hair is trimmed short at the sides and the back of the head. The top hat continues to be worn for formal day and evening wear, but the felt Homburg and derby generally replace it for business wear. The straw Panama hat and the flat-brimmed boater hat are most popular in the summer. Golf and sporting occasions call for the soft, billed cap.

Neck/Shoulder/Arm

Although the high starched collar is still worn, the softer, turned-down shirt collar takes over for most business and sports outfits. A four-in-hand or Windsor tie usually accompanies these softer-collared shirts. Jackets have lightly padded shoulders, medium-width lapels, and a slightly narrow shape. Standard wear through most of the decade is the three-piece suit with matching vest. It is popular in dark colors and in checks.

Waist/Hip/Trousers

Trouser legs are tapered to a narrow cut at the ankle. The waistline is flat and without pleats. Trousers have creases center front and back, and cuffs below the ankle. The hip is generally flat, and the waistline is normal.

Footwear

Although high-top shoes are still in favor, the lower cut oxford shoe takes over as the predominant business wear during this decade. This is especially true after World War I.

1920s

1920–1929

Headdress/Hair
Bobbed or shingled hairstyles are cut short to the nape of the neck, are ear-length, and worn close to the head. The cloche hat, fitted close to the head and covering the ears, is popular through the middle of the decade. It usually has a small turned-back brim. In the early 1920s a wider brimmed picture hat with a deep crown appears with day dresses. Earrings are popular with the new short hairstyles.

Neck/Shoulder/Arm
Short hairstyles emphasize the length of the neck. Necklines are usually round or V shaped. Shoulders are soft and curved into a long torso with flattened bustline. Sleeveless, short-sleeved, and long-sleeved dresses all have a soft shoulder line. Most sleeves are cut straight. Costume jewelry becomes fashionable for the first time. Women wear long strands of pearls and beads, which reach almost to the waist, with these low-waisted dresses.

Waist/Hip/Skirt
The dropped waistline extends from the top of the hipbone to just above the thigh and helps achieve the long, flat boyish look. The dropped waistline aims to deemphasize the hips. The skirt reaches from the hip to below the knee in 1926 and from the hip to the lower calf at the beginning and at the end of the decade. The skirt stays close to the body and takes on many shapes, from pleated to bias-cut handkerchief hems. When the hemline rises to below the knee for the first time, stockings take on a new importance. They are light-colored silk hose with seams running up the back of the leg.

Footwear
The pump, a low-cut, slip-on shoe, and the famous T-strap shoe of the 1920s have a 2" or higher spool or Louis heel. Many varieties of strapped pumps are available, and a lace-up walking shoe with a lower heel is also popular.

1920s

1920–1929

Headdress/Hair

Side-parted hairstyles are short around the ears and at the back of the head. Some hairstyles are slicked down with pomade to achieve a "patent leather" look. Many hat styles are available, including the flat-brimmed straw boater for sportswear and the top hat for evening. Also available are the felt derby for formal daywear, the softer brimmed fedora for business dress, and the brimmed cloth cap for a sporting look.

Neck/Shoulder/Arm

Men wear shirts with soft collars except for formal evening dress, when a stiff winged-tip collar is still the proper wear. The four-in-hand tie is medium in width and knotted at the front of the shirt. The ascot scarf and the bow tie are also popular. The shoulder line is narrow in men's suits, lapels are medium to narrow in width, and shoulder padding is small. Most men wear single-breasted, three-button suits with matching trousers, vest, and jacket. Blazers and sport jackets become more popular. The sleeve is straight and has a small vent and three buttons at the end.

Waist/Hip/Trousers

Most suit jackets are hip-length and worn with creased, cuffed trousers that are slender in cut. Knickers called plus fours and flannel trousers called Oxford bags have pleats at the waist and are fuller through the leg.

Footwear

A lace-up oxford with a flat heel is the most common shoe. It comes in black, brown, navy, tan, and a combination light and dark two-tone shoe. The work shoe is a high-top, lace-up shoe that ends above the ankle. Rubber-soled canvas tennis shoes start to become popular.

1930s

1930–1939

Headdress/Hair

Hairstyles for the 1930s are close to the head, parted on the side, and styled in finger waves. Most styles are short, ending just below the ear, Between 1936 and 1939 hair is more often swept back at the top of the head into rolls at the side, with the lower part of the hair pulled back into a roll or bun. Hats have small or wide brims and round crowns. The smaller hats tilt to one side of the head. A version of the male fedora becomes popular at the end of the decade when a more tailored look comes into style.

Neck/Shoulder/Arm

The natural body shape of the 1930s has a soft bustline and shoulders. Many garments are bias cut to give a soft, clinging flow of fabric around the body. Cropped fabrics and silk fibers enhance this soft body look. The soft shoulder line of 1931 develops into small shoulder pads by 1938. Most sleeves are straight on day dresses and suits, and evening wear shows bare arms and even bare backs. Some sleeves puff on the upper arm and taper to a fitted sleeve on the lower arm. Necklines vary from round to V-shaped and later include blouses and suits with tailored lapels. Scarves are a major neck accessory. Day and evening wear includes gloves. The clutch purse is a favorite accessory. Many types of sportswear are available, including the first two-piece swimsuit.

Waist/Hip/Skirt

A slightly raised waistline, about 1" or 2" above a normal waistline, is usually accented with a belt or waistline seam. Most dresses fasten with a side-waist zipper or hooks. The hips are flat and slender like the bustline. Some skirts flare below the hip or around the knee. Skirt lengths are below the knee to midcalf. Stockings are silk or cotton, with seams up the center back.

Footwear

Medium-height pumps with a thick heel are worn. The toe is round, and open-toe shoes appear in the last half of the decade. Two-tone shoes appear, and women wear strapped sandals with a heel for evening.

1930s

1930–1939

Headdress/Hair

Men's hair is parted in the center or on the side and cut short around the ears and at the back of the head. Hair is frequently longer on top and combed straight back or slicked down on the sides. The fedora with a medium brim is the most popular hat. Sports and informal outdoor headwear consists of soft, billed caps.

Neck/Shoulder/Arm

The white shirt with soft collar and Windsor tie is standard male dress. Ties are made in printed and striped patterns. Men wear scarves at the neck of blazers and sport jackets. The turtleneck, or polo-neck, sweater is also available for sporting wear. Suit coats and jackets have medium shoulder pads and a medium-width lapel. They are single- or double-breasted. The sleeve is straight, with two or three buttons at the wrist vent. Waistcoats, or vests, are available but not mandatory for proper dress as they were earlier. Short-sleeved sport shirts make their first appearance during the 1930s.

Waist/Hip/Trousers

Squarer cut jackets are also wider through the shoulders, and this width continues to the hips. Trousers, pleated at the waist, have a fuller, baggier look and a 2" to 2 $\frac{1}{2}$" turned-up cuff where they break on the shoe. Knickers are available for outdoor wear with a vest, coat, and tie.

Footwear

The oxford lace-up shoe is standard male footwear. Men wear two-toned shoes and light-colored shoes for summer, and dark oxfords for winter. The first slip-on loafer becomes available during this decade. The canvas-top, rubber-soled shoe becomes increasingly popular, as do sandals for pool and recreational wear.

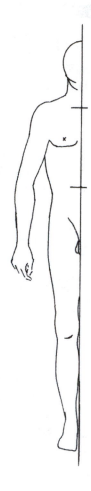

1940s

1940–1949

Headdress/Hair

Familiar hairstyles of the 1940s include the page-boy, a side-parted style with hair rolled under from below and ear to shoulder-length. The upswept style has a type of French roll at the back of the head. Hair is also rolled up over padding at each side of the head, creating height at the sides, and the lower hair is pulled into a bun at the back of the head. Hats are abundant and available in many styles. Turbans, berets, wide-brimmed straw and felt hats, tall-crowned fedoras, and snoods or hoods are worn. Feathers and wide ribbons, and especially veils are popular as trimming.

Neck/Shoulder/Arm

The shoulder line takes on a wide look from 1940 to 1946 with shoulder pads and wide lapels on women's suits and coats. Softer crepe dresses and evening gowns also have shoulder padding. In 1947 the Dior "new look" has a softer shoulder line. Necklines vary, but the tailored look with collar and lapels is seen often. Sleeves are straight and long or three-quarter-length. The bustline is raised, with a rounded look. Darts extend from the waist to below the bustline to emphasize this shape.

Waist/Hip/Skirt

The waistline cinches in with a girdle, and the hips are smooth and flat. The waistline is of normal height, and skirt length varies above and below the knee during the war years. The "new look" that is introduced after the war drops hemlines to the mid-calf for the rest of the decade. Four-gored skirts flare from below the hip to the hemline. This style is flat at the waist and widens as it gets longer. Straight skirts also become popular after 1947.

Footwear

The high-heeled pump comes in many versions with open toes and open heels, platform soles, and strappy sandals. The heel is slightly narrower than in the l930s but wider than the shoe of the l950s. The toe is round. Casual and sportswear includes sandals and lace-up walking shoes.

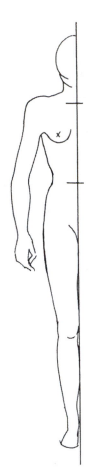

1940s

1940–1949

Headdress/Hair

Hair is short, and usually parted on the side. It is slightly longer on the top and combed to the side. The fedora takes on a wider brim and tilts to one side of the head, or with the brim slanted to one side. Military uniforms include many types of head-dress during the war years.

Neck/Shoulder/Arm

The shoulders take on extra-wide shoulder pads, and jackets have a square shape. They are single- or double-breasted, and stripes and checks are popular. The collar of the shirt and the necktie take on brighter colors and become wider. The ties of this period are famous for their prints and wide cut. Bow ties for day wear are popular in brighter colors and prints.

After 1947 the shoulder width lessens as fashion heads for a transition in the 1950s. Long-sleeved dress shirts, ties, and suits are standard business wear. Short-sleeved sport shirts appear in bright prints. Summer sport jackets in prints and checks accompany light-colored slacks. Vests are seldom seen.

Waist/Hip/Trousers

Trousers, pleated at the front waist, are cut wider, creating fuller looking hips and pants. Trousers match suit coats, but sport jackets and slacks become equally acceptable for business wear. Trousers have wide turned-up cuffs at the hem. After 1947 the silhouette narrows slightly.

Footwear

The lace-up oxford in brown or black is the standard shoe. It has a thicker sole than the shoe of the 1950s. Men still wear sandals and two-tone spectator shoes for more casual occasions.

1950s

1950–1959

Headdress/Hair

Hair is short and worn close to the head. A favorite haircut is the poodle cut, a layered hairstyle that is short and wavy. Other styles include the French twist, a vertical roll at the back of the head. Longer hair comes into fashion during the late 1950s, and styles include the ponytail. Hats vary from the wide-brimmed picture hat with a turned-in brim to the turban-type hat in the shape of a fez. At the start of the decade, hats include the pillbox, with floral trim and a short veil, and a cloche hat reminiscent of the 1920s.

Neck/Shoulder/Arm

The shoulderline becomes narrower in the 1950s. A raised bustline with a cone-shaped bra gives a new shape to the female chest. The tailored suits of the early 1950s have narrow lapels and sleeves. Evening dress of this period is famous for the strapless gown with bare shoulders. The chemise dress of the mid-1950s is sleeveless or has short or three-quarter sleeves.

Waist/Hip/Skirt

The tightly cinched waistline creates an hourglass look. Suits have narrow, slender skirts. Day and evening dresses may have very full skirts supported by stiffened petticoats called crinolines. Belts are popular and emphasize the nipped-in waist. Skirt lengths stay about 2" below the knee for most of the decade. The chemise dress, cut straight and without a waistline, is introduced toward the end of this period. Another new style is the A-line or trapeze dress, which has a skirt that flares from under the bustline to the hem. Sheer nylon stockings with a seamed back emphasize the leg, and seamless stockings appear for the first time.

Footwear

Pointed toes and pencil-thin stiletto or spike heels are the hallmark of 1950s pumps. Flat-styled shoes include an abundance of ballet-type slippers, the loafer, and canvas tennis shoes. Thick white socks called bobby sox are worn with these shoes.

1950s

1950–1959

Headdress/Hair

Hairstyles vary from the very short crew cut, which is almost a shaved head, to longer sideburns and hair curling at the nape of the neck. This latter style features a wave of hair at the front, parted on the side, and has hair combed into a point at the back of the head. In-between styles include side-parted hair that is short at the sides and back, with some additional length on the top. The fedora is the most popular business hat and has a narrower brim to match the narrower proportions of the suit. Many men wear the flat-top, brimmed hat. Sporting occasions call for many styles of billed caps.

Neck/Shoulder/Arm

The jacket shoulder line has smaller shoulder pads and a narrower cut from shoulders through the body. Lapels are narrower, and most suits are single-breasted and often made of gray flannel. Ties also become thinner, ranging from 1 1/2" to 2" in width, about half the width of the 1940s ties. Most ties are solid, and knit ties become available. Shirts are white, light blue, and pink, and most have button-down collars. Striped shirts also come into fashion. Sport jackets are made of a range of fabrics from corduroy to madras and plaids. Two-button suits replace many of the three-button styles.

Waist/Hip/Trousers

The trousers are flat across the hips and belted, without pleats at the waist. They are narrower, as are the cuffs at the ankle. Beltless, cuffless trousers come into fashion during the late 1950s. Some more flamboyant styles feature very tight, fitted trousers or jeans that end above the ankle. Bermuda shorts, full shorts in bright printed fabrics that end at the knee, are favored for sportswear.

Footwear

Loafers and other slip-on shoes increase in popularity. The younger generation wears crepe-soled shoes, two-tone saddle shoes, canvas tennis shoes, and white buckskin shoes. New Italian shoes with slightly pointed toes are introduced during the second half of the decade.

1960s

1960–1969

Headdress/Hair

The 1960s are a tumultuous decade, with great charges from the bouffant hairstyles of the early part of the decade to the long, straight, and geometric styles of the latter part. A teased hairstyle, the beehive, attains great height. The Jackie Kennedy pillbox hat and some "helmet" styles are part of the early 1960s look, though hats tend to be out of fashion in a rebellion against the "proper" 1950s.

Neck/Shoulder/Arm

The shoulder and neckline tend to be round and soft. The flat or natural-shaped bustline is the ideal. Bras lose all the padding and shaping of the 1950s and adopt a natural body shape. In the late 1960s some women go without bras to carry the natural shape to the ultimate. Many fashions are sleeveless. Dresses and suits have long and short sleeves. Blouses and vests in beaded, embroidered, and fringed styles make up the dress of the "flower children."

Waist/Hip/Skirt/Slacks

The waistline fluctuates from the high Empire style to no waist in the A-line dress. Blue jeans, slacks, and skirts fasten on the hip, several inches below the waist. The hip is the focus of these hip hugger fashions, which are usually accented with long and decorative belts. Most jeans flare below the knee in a style called bell-bottoms. The hip is slender, and slacks and jeans dominate female dress as much as skirts for the first time. In the last half of the decade the miniskirt becomes high fashion as the hemline reaches the mid-thigh for the first time. Short skirts are complemented by patterned stockings and opaque tights.

Footwear

Leather, suede, and plastic boots accompany both daytime and evening fashions. Some boots are light in color, even white; others are darker. Most are ankle to knee height and zip or lace up the front or side. Shoes have low, square heels and round toes. Pumps are frequently worn with A-line dresses. Jeans universally appear with sandals.

1960s

1960–1969

Headdress/Hair

For the first time since Louis XIV men wear shoulder-length hair. Conservative males still wear short, side-parted styles. Some men wear hair that brushes the top of the collar; other men's hair reaches to the shoulder, and sometimes the midchest. Caps, like the soft, billed Beatle cap, create a younger look. A very narrow-brimmed fedora accompanies business suits.

Neck/Shoulder/Arm

Men's suits have slightly padded shoulders, medium lapels, slightly curved-in waist and sides, and center back vents. Single-breasted suits fasten with two-button front closings. The tie is also of medium width. Shirts are white, colored, and have large flowered prints. Hippie styles include large full-sleeved shirts in bright colors and prints with fringed or embroidered vests. The Nehru jacket, which buttons up to the neck with a standing collar, is in style for a short period.

Waist/Hip/Trousers

Business suits have a normal waistline, but jeans and slacks from the mid-1960s on have a dropped waist. These pants belt at the top of the hip. They have a tight fit through the hips and thigh and flare or bell out below the knee. Bell-bottom pants often fall past the ankle and over the top of the shoe. Business trousers remain straight and cuffless.

Footwear

Shoes range from a standard dress oxford to boots in suede and leather that reach the ankle or the knee. Boots usually zip on the side and have a 2" square heel. At the end of the decade toes start to become squarer.

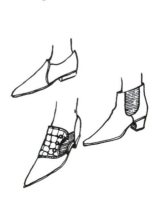

Chapter 7

Creating a Portfolio

Overview

A designer needs a portfolio to present his or her designs for work or graduate school interviews. It allows you to put your material together in a fast and easy presentation for prospective employers or schools. Although interviewers look for different qualities in a portfolio, you generally want to show quality, flexibility, and varieties of work, plus working sketches and research to show the process involved.

The overall goal of the portfolio is to present your best work and make a positive impression on the interviewer. It is important that your work be clean in presentation, follow some form of logical progression, and be easy to see. The portfolio must also be manageable: you may need to carry it a distance while walking, or you may need to take it on a train or airplane. The "fashion" of creating a portfolio does change from time to time, but the following arc some basics.

Costume Sketches

Number of Pieces

If you participate in the University Resident Theater Association (URTA) or graduate school interviews, the interviewer may dictate the number of sketches you may present. In any case, it is a good idea to limit your portfolio because most interviews have strict time limits. One strategy is to show two to four sketches from each show or project to illustrate character relationships and continuity of style. Plan on ten or twelve pieces to show your best work. You can have additional work available if there is time to present it.

Variety

You obviously want to present what you consider your best work. You also want to show both period and modern dress, low- and high-budget productions, and realistic and stylized designs if possible. Demonstrate that you can do more than one style of design. Show sketches done on both a high and a low budget.

It is important to have fabric and trim swatches on every sketch. These swatches should be 3" to 6" in length and about 2" in width so they are easy to see. Arrange them in the proportions in which they appear on the costume. Even if you have not executed the designs or if they are from a class project, it is still important to include fabric swatches. Be sure they are as close as possible to the color and texture of the sketch. Include dye swatches and any samples of fabric modification, such as aging or painting. Sketches of wigs, jewelry, or accessories are valuable additions.

Budget/Prices

Know the cost of the finished costume for each sketch in your portfolio. Interviewers often ask about prices. If you do not know the exact cost, estimate as accurately as possible. Also know the price of fabric per yard and how much fabric a costume requires. Include in your repertory the total cost of the show and the cost of individual items such as shoes, millinery, and other accessories, and of all undergarments such as corsets, petticoats, tights, and padding. These items may be available in stock, but you must know what the cost would be if they were to be built.

Photographs

Photographs of finished work are just as important as costume sketches. The photos should be of the finished costume and should be 8" × 10". The colors shown in the photos should be as close to the sketch and fabric swatches as possible. In your portfolio place the photo beside or across from the costume sketch so it is easy to view them together. Have at least six or eight photographs of finished work if possible.

Research

It is good to include a bibliography, photocopies of research material, color plots, action charts, or other homework material used in the preparation of a costume sketch. Include preliminary drawings to show the thought process and the original ideas for one or two of the designs in your portfolio.

Presentation

Try to place all work either vertically or horizontally in your portfolio so it need not be turned as it is viewed. Most interviewers do not want sketches matted or covered with acetate. They prefer to see work in its original state because acetate distorts color and line, although only minutely. Lay out your sketches, photos, and other material in a format that can be easily viewed.

Begin the portfolio with your strongest design work. After costume designs, you may present wigs, jewelry, masks, or other items you have designed or executed. It is also refreshing to include a few selections from drawing, color, photography, or other art classes you have taken. Do not include drawings other than your own or costumes you have patterned or stitched unless they are clearly labeled as such. They belong in a separate production portfolio.

Practice

Lastly, practice a portfolio presentation in front of friends, teachers, or other designers to help your concentration and flow of ideas become more natural. They can give you feedback about what is clear or unclear, and it will help you be more relaxed when the actual interview takes place. This is a chance to time the presentation if it needs to meet precise time requirements. For example, an interview may be limited to ten minutes, and you want to be sure you can present your strongest work in that amount of time. Know your concepts, your characters, and how they have been adapted to your production. Try to relax. Be positive. You are presenting yourself as well as your portfolio.

Figure 7.1 Actual costume illustrations by Georgia O'Daniel Baker from *The Three Sisters*. Note the material swatches in the corner.

Figure 7.2 Costume illustration by Georgia O'Daniel Baker from *H.M.S. Pinafore*.

Figure 7.3 Costume illustration by Georgia O'Daniel
Baker from *H.M.S. Pinafore*.

Figure 7.4 Costume illustrations by Georgia O'Daniel
Baker from *Once Upon a Mattress*.

Bibliography

Albers, Josef. *Interaction of Color*. New Haven: Yale University Press, 1963.

Arnold, Janet. *Patterns of Fashion 2*. New York: Drama Book Publishers, 1966.

Black, J. Anderson, and Garland, Madge. *A History of Fashion*. New York: William Morrow and Co., 1980.

Blum, Stella. *Everyday Fashions of the Thirties*. New York: Dover Publications, Inc., 1986.

Blum, Stella. *Everyday Fashions of the Twenties*. New York: Dover Publications, Inc.. 1981.

Ewing, Elizabeth. *Dress and Undress*. London: B .T. Batsford, Ltd., 1978.

Gillon, Edmund Vincent, Jr. *The Gibson Girl and Her America: The Best Drawings of Charles Dana Gibson*. New York: Dover Publications, Inc., 1969.

Hall, Carolyn. *The Twenties in Vogue*. New York: Harmony Books, 1983.

Hill, Margot Hamilton, and Bucknell, Peter A. *The Evolution of Fashion: Pattern and Cut from 1066 to 1930*. New York: Drama Book Publishers, 1967.

Ingham, Rosemary, and Covey, Liz. *The Costume Designer's Handbook*. Englewood Cliffs, NJ: Prentice-Hall, 1983.

Itten, Joannes. *The Elements of Color*. New York: Van Nostrand Reinhold Company, 1970.

Itten, Joannes. *The Art of Color*. New York: Van Nostrand Reinhold Company, 1961 and 1973.

Moore, Doris Langley. *Fashion through Fashion Plates 1771–1970*. New York: Clarkson N. Potter, Inc., 1971.

Nunn, Joan. *Fashion in Costume 1200–1980*. London: The Herbert Press, 1984.

Robinson, Julian. *Fashion in the Forties*. London: Academy Editions, 1976.

Russell, Douglas A. *Costume History and Style*. Englewood Cliffs, NJ: Prentice-Hall, 1983.

Russell, Douglas A. *Period Style for the Theater*. Boston: Allyn and Bacon, Inc., 1980.

Russell, Douglas A. *Stage Costume Design*. Englewood Cliffs, N.J.: Prentice-Hall, 1985.

Selbie, Robert. *The Anatomy of Fashion*. New York: Crescent Books, Crown Publishers, 1977.

Tortora, Phyllis, and Eubank, Keith. *A Survey of Historic Costume*. New York: Fairchild Publications, 1989.

Tyrrell, Anne V. *Changing Trends in Fashion*. London: B.T. Batsford, Ltd., 1986.

Warren, Geoffrey. *Fashion Accessories Since 1500*. New York: Drama Book Publishers, 1987.

Watson, Philip J. *Costume of Old Testament Peoples*. Edgemont, Pa.: Chelsea House Publishers, 1987.

Waugh, Norah. *Corsets and Crinolines*. New York: Theatre Arts Books, 1954.

Waugh, Norah. *The Cut of Men's Clothes 1600–1900*. London: Faber and Faber Ltd., 1964.

Waugh, Norah. *The Cut of Women's Clothes 1600–1930*. New York: Theatre Arts Books, 1968.

Wilcox, R. Turner. *The Mode in Costume*. New York: Charles Scribner's Sons, 1958.

Wilcox, R. Turner. *The Mode in Footwear*. New York: Charles Scribner's Sons, 1948.

Wilcox, R. Turner. *The Mode in Hats and Headdress*. New York: Charles Scribner's Sons, 1945.

Worrell, Estelle Ansley. *American Costume 1840–1920*. Harrisburg, PA: Stackpole Books, 1979.

Index